RESPONDING
TO RAPID CHANGE
IN LIBRARIES

RESPONDING TO RAPID CHANGE IN LIBRARIES
A User Experience Approach

CALLAN BIGNOLI AND LAUREN STARA

ALA
Editions
CHICAGO   2021

CALLAN BIGNOLI is the director of the library at Olin College of Engineering in Needham, Massachusetts. She gathers inspiration from everywhere to inform user-centered practices and push the profession forward. Callan studies and speaks about user experience design, library management, and social issues in technology, challenging students and colleagues to fight for a more just and human future.

LAUREN STARA is a library building specialist with the Massachusetts Board of Library Commissioners, helping public libraries around the Commonwealth improve their physical spaces. A registered architect and a librarian, she has worked in and/or consulted for libraries in eight US states, three Canadian provinces, and three Eastern European countries. She has taught at library schools in Canada and Bulgaria, and she speaks and presents frequently on library design, design thinking, and service design.

Portions of Chapters 2 and 5 originally appeared as posts to *Public Libraries Online*, http://publiclibrariesonline.org, between August 2016 and February 2017. Used with permission.

ISBNs
978-0-8389-4835-4 (paper)
978-0-8389-4838-5 (PDF)
978-0-8389-4978-8 (ePub)
978-0-8389-4976-4 (Kindle)

Library of Congress Control Number: 2020030360

Text design in the Chaparral, Gotham, and Bell Gothic typefaces.
Cover design by Kimberly Thornton.

♾ This paper meets the requirements of ANSI/NISO Z39.48-1992 (Permanence of Paper).

Printed in the United States of America
25 24 23 22 21   5 4 3 2 1

Contents

Acknowledgments

Our book's structure draws inspiration from the iconic lions flanking the New York Public Library's central branch (Patience and Fortitude), adding in a third "lion" (Passion) to round out attributes necessary to embrace and respond to rapid change.

Thanks to Andrea Bunker, who provided guidance and support in the early drafts of this book.

Callan: Thanks to my family, who always knew I'd write a book sooner or later.

Lauren: Thanks to Chris Painter, who started me down this road.

Introduction

Why This Book?

As we wrapped up the manuscript for this book, it was May 2020, months into an unprecedented global health crisis with far-reaching consequences we still can't comprehend. The outbreak of the highly contagious novel coronavirus disease COVID-19 closed countless businesses and organizations—gyms, bars, restaurants, movie theaters, retail stores, college campuses, and thousands of libraries. Surging unemployment and market volatility were devastating the economic prospects of millions of Americans, from new graduates to service workers who were prohibited from doing their jobs. Huge budget shortfalls were projected for every state. We're still only at the beginning of a long crawl back to normalcy, and we don't have a clue how this will reshape our own lives, let alone the trajectory of our profession.

We wrote the majority of this book long before the first rumblings of COVID-19 came onto the radar in the United States, and at first it seemed like there was no possible way what we had written could stand up to the expectations of a book about change in libraries published during a pandemic. But as we reread the draft in preparation for sending it off to our editor, we realized that the motivation that drove us before the beginning of this year is the same motivation that will keep us going in response to the new world we'll be living and working in by the time this book is published.

Patience and Fortitude are the lions that flank the front steps of the New York Public Library's main branch on 5th Avenue in Manhattan. Their iconic grace is emblematic of the calm and strength needed to guide change. We pulled in a third imaginary lion, Passion, to guide the change we write about in book. The book's structure was sketched out long before we knew where we'd be in 2021, but it feels even more relevant now. Passion, patience, and fortitude are what will keep our heads in the game as we confront the challenges that we're already facing in the aftermath of COVID-19.

As for our own passion, patience, and fortitude, we are both dedicated to libraries as an institution. Both of us have spent years working in all kinds of libraries: public, academic, and special. One thing that all of them struggle with is constant change.

Why? On the one hand, librarianship has deep roots as a rules-based profession. Librarians make order and organization where there was none before. We like consistency because it makes things more findable for patrons and makes our work lives easier. On the other hand, we are often scraping by without enough staff, funding, or time to do everything our communities need from us. Because of that scarcity, it can be hard to prepare for uncharted territory when we're barely feeling able to stick to the current map.

We have come to understand that rather than just being disruptive and difficult, change can also be an incredible force for good. Learning to embrace change—making it a thread that runs through and informs everything we do—can invigorate our libraries and our lives. Sure, the process can be challenging and sometimes a little scary, but it's also inspiring and really fun.

Our goal with this book is to talk about embracing change as a constant in libraries and librarianship. As we navigate the impacts of COVID-19, we think these strategies are more important than ever. In part I, "Passion," we'll start at a more philosophical level by explaining the mind-set we're suggesting you bring to this work. Next, in part II, "Patience," we'll move to applying that mind-set to specific topics ranging from hiring practices to security concerns and from technology to physical space. Finally, in part III, "Fortitude," we'll examine how to problem-solve and manage projects while contending with constant change and discuss the threats and opportunities that await us as a field in a transforming world.

CHANGE

The library is a growing organism.

—S. R. Ranganathan

Constant change is nothing new. However, it's a fact that we are living in a time of accelerated change, and libraries, despite their traditional image as history's gatekeepers and preservationists, are along for the ride. The ways people seek and consume information have become very different in the past two decades, and they will continue to evolve quickly in response to technological and cultural developments.

Over the past fifty years, technology has become the backbone for public library services. Online information has largely replaced print for rapidly changing information, such as government documents and research and developments in medicine, science, and technology. Libraries will continue to need to adapt to new technologies, and this means incorporating as much flexibility into services as well as buildings, furniture, and equipment as possible.

Patron expectations are now shaped by megacorporations such as Amazon, Starbucks, and Netflix. Public spaces are becoming increasingly scarce, and in many urban centers in the United States, rents are skyrocketing while housing options are shrinking. The cost of living and the weight of debt are crushing people's ability to accumulate expendable income. This impacts how Americans are spending their leisure time as they seek room, equipment, and supplies to explore new hobbies and interests beyond what they can afford (or have room for) in their own homes; this trend was highlighted during the COVID-19 pandemic in 2020. In order to remain relevant and respond to emergent needs, libraries are shifting their service models to become more nimble, expansive, and adaptable to these cultural shifts.

So, how can we write a book about constant change that, once it's published and printed, will instantly render itself unchangeable? The web designer and writer Erin Kissane states this in her book *The Elements of Content Strategy*, a treatise on keeping websites well-curated and usable: "If newspapers are 'dead tree media,' information published online is a live green plant." Libraries and their collections are live green plants, too, and as Kissane writes, "Plants are more useful if we tend them and shape their futures to suit our goals." We've done our best to write this book in a way that will help you tend your live green libraries, making them more useful as you work to shape their future and reach your goals.

Andrew K. Pace's *The Ultimate Digital Library*, an ALA Editions title published in 2003, focuses on the anxieties that struck librarians when the internet as we know it began to reshape society. It was a useful read as we were writing this book, giving us a frame of reference for the strange ways that technologies change and yet also manage to remain the same. Pace wrote then about problems we still have today—overpriced academic literature, lack of usability in software interfaces, and pressure from Google and Amazon, just to name a few.

Pace identified the biggest challenge to libraries in 2003 as something he calls "disintermediation," a trend toward libraries and librarians being taken out of the process of finding and providing information. While some might try to argue that Google and Amazon have won that battle, libraries are so much more than information service providers. We'd say one of the biggest challenges to libraries today is figuring out all the ways in which we can go above and beyond that role while still keeping our core values and goals of inclusion, equal access, and community in mind. We hope this book will help you find a clear path forward in the face of constant change.

NOTES

1. Erin Kissane, *The Elements of Content Strategy* (New York: A Book Apart, 2010), 12.
2. Kissane, *Elements of Content Strategy*, 12.
3. Andrew K. Pace, *The Ultimate Digital Library* (Chicago: ALA Editions, 2003).

PART I
Passion

Why did you choose to work in a library? We'd guess it's at least in part because you want to help people and give them access to the resources they want and need. This book is grounded in user experience principles, attitudes, and practices. We'll start with a crash course in how user-centered design connects us to our patrons and aligns our goals with their own. These concepts will help you connect your passion for libraries to simple, concrete ways of making it real.

1
Customer Service Expectations in the Twenty-First Century

L ibraries are responding to changing user needs by shifting their service model to become more nimble and adaptable. Customer service expectations, in libraries as much as everywhere else, are shaped by a handful of tech and retail corporations with outsized influence on American life. It's not easy for libraries to stay competitive and responsive in areas where those companies are fighting them for ground.

To break that down a bit more, paid services like Amazon's Kindle Unlimited and Audible provide easy access to e-books and audiobooks for a monthly fee; Spotify and Netflix provide streaming services for music and television. People subscribe to digital editions of magazines and newspapers, often without realizing their local library is already paying for the same subscription. In libraries, we can request books and articles we don't own on behalf of our users with a turnaround time that's not half bad, but people accustomed to overnight delivery might get tired of waiting and opt to buy or illegally download the material.

Aside from these content concerns, libraries have long served their role as a *third place*, the term sociologists use for the social areas in life outside home and work. But this third place could also be a coffee shop or a social media site. Any way you slice it, whatever you attribute it to, patrons have higher expectations of their libraries. More and different types of space are required to offer the types of programming and services that have become increasingly standard in recent years, such as quiet and collaborative study spaces, creation or tinkering spaces of various types, community meeting spaces, and self-service options. As if that isn't enough pressure, the ways people seek and consume information are not static. They will continue to evolve quickly in response to technological and cultural developments. In turn, libraries need to constantly adapt to new technologies and service expectations, and this means that flexibility and community needs must be at the foundation of every decision.

If we peer outside of librarianship, much of the current research about customer service expectations—and other aspects of marketing and business in the digital age—puts an inordinate focus on the preferences of millennials. Of course, we're not serving only millennials—and we never were—not to mention the whole generation of young adults that follows them now. A 2015 report from Nuance Communications, a software company that builds voice recognition and automated phone systems, shows that there's not so much of a difference between generations when it comes to what people expect and what frustrates them.[1] Members of different generations reported unified frustration when they couldn't reach a "real person" at the end of a phone call or e-mail transaction. They also reported an equal adoption of self-service options and agreed that self-service has generally improved customer service quality. All of this is relevant to libraries, as we invest in self-checkout machines and explore the possibility of staffless hours or branches.

We've found there's much to be learned from other types of service organizations and the dimensions of customer service they're finding to be most important today. While the end goals or services they're offering might be totally different, libraries have analogous touchpoints that can be just as important in determining their perceived success or failure as service providers.

Take airlines, for example. A 2017 article in the *Journal of Air Transport Management* notes that customers of Aegean Airlines were most satisfied with the company's quick self-service option for online check-in.[2] Those same customers reported that it was most important to them to be able to get on their way as quickly as possible upon landing, whether it's to a connecting flight or a taxi into town, with minimal confusion or slowdowns. Interestingly, the most satisfying part and the most important part of the service journey were identified as two different things. What might the most satisfying and most important parts of the library service journey be? Are these the same for everyone? How might they change?

Another industry to peer into is hospitality. In a 2019 article published in the journal *Tourism Management*, a group of researchers describes how hotel visitors' expectations change over time when they stay at a hotel more than once.[3] They found that room quality and appearance are most important for a first stay and that good service becomes increasingly important during second and third stays. For these repeat visitors, service quality is the most important factor in decisions to revisit, beating out cleanliness and hotel location. How might libraries rise to the challenge of increased service expectations of their repeat patrons?

All trends, in libraries and everywhere else, are impermanent and subject to their own evolution. As Generation Z members take over the spotlight from millennials, what new insights will we discover? Will the fact that they grew up in the time of social media mean everything about serving them must change, or will their needs be largely the same as for the cohorts that came before? And how can libraries meaningfully compete on all of these fronts and keep up with this constant evolution?

We need to begin to adopt the mind-set that is comfortable with asking these questions. We can break down these big challenges into smaller chunks and be honest with ourselves about what our libraries can do better. We can ask our patrons to tell us what's working and what isn't. We can shore up our self-service options and work to make those experiences as frictionless as we'd want getting a boarding pass to be. We can think of ways to make it easy to get out of the library and back on the road when people drop by and expect to be in and out in just a second. Clearer signage, posted information about transportation options, and easier parking can all contribute to that. How can we make first-time patrons come back again? We can be approachable and attentive not only in our interactions with all patrons but also when crafting resources and road maps about our services online and in the building. We can focus on establishing our brand both when patrons first come in to register for their library cards and out in the community where they are already learning, living, and working.

REFERENCE SERVICES: THE DE FACTO GENIUS BAR

In 2001 Apple launched its first Genius Bar, an in-person tech support hub for the company's brick-and-mortar retail stores (see figure 1.1). Since then, these service points have evolved to include the Studio, a classroom of sorts staffed by trainers who show visitors how to use various Apple software and peripherals. Meanwhile, reference desks in public libraries around the world have become the de facto Genius Bars for technologies of all makes and models, including Apple's. There are 271 Apple Stores[4] and over 16,500 public library branches[5] in the United States. Reference staff field questions all day long about how to use the technology that's already in the library, not to mention the hodgepodge of different devices that patrons bring with them. And unlike the Apple Store, the library isn't tucked away in a fancy suburban mall and has no intention of selling you an $800 tablet.

FIGURE 1.1
Launched in 2001, Apple's in-store Genius Bars provide personalized face-to-face tech support for the company's products.

The questions that come to reference staff range from the very library-specific ("How do I borrow e-books on my Kindle?") to ones that aren't really being answered in any other public place ("What are the privacy risks of using Facebook?"). They can be as simple as a request to replace paper in the copier or as complex as asking for advanced training on 3-D printing software. The tech-savviness of patrons varies widely, just as it does for staff. We have some pointers for how to handle this influx of technology questions and a reminder: we're not likely to see this trend slow down anytime soon.

- Offer a variety of choices for patrons looking for tech help aside from reference interactions. Many libraries have seen success with bookable one-on-one sessions that give patrons a chance for more uninterrupted time with a helpful person who can assist with troubleshooting, accessing online resources, or building new skills. This model is especially beneficial for tech novices who might feel pressured or uncomfortable in a group learning setting. That being said, some people prefer to learn alongside others in a classroom format. These trainings should be offered at multiple times throughout the week to accommodate patrons' schedules.
- If you or your staff feel uncomfortable with technology or with playing the role of expert in these one-on-one, on-desk, or classroom settings, try to unpack why. Are you promising something that your team might not be able to deliver (i.e., training for a very specialized or complicated program)? You can say no to requests that are truthfully outside your area of expertise. Have you not used the technologies people are asking about? You could set up a "petting zoo" where you and staff have a hands-on opportunity to try out technology before working with a patron. Do you feel like you have to know everything about an app or a device before you offer training on it? Think of your training as an opportunity not to clutch the expert role but instead say, "I don't know, but let's find out together."

Providing technology help is not so very different from answering a more traditional reference question that requires you to find credible resources on a

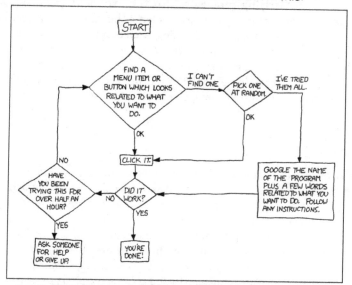

DEAR VARIOUS PARENTS, GRANDPARENTS, CO-WORKERS, AND OTHER "NOT COMPUTER PEOPLE."

WE DON'T MAGICALLY KNOW HOW TO DO EVERYTHING IN EVERY PROGRAM. WHEN WE HELP YOU, WE'RE USUALLY JUST DOING THIS:

PLEASE PRINT THIS FLOWCHART OUT AND TAPE IT NEAR YOUR SCREEN. CONGRATULATIONS; YOU'RE NOW THE LOCAL COMPUTER EXPERT!

FIGURE 1.2
This XKCD Comic #627, "Tech Support Cheat Sheet," offers indispensable advice for today's reference desks.

topic you've never heard about before the minute you're consulted about it. Just as in that situation, take the time to listen to and understand the question. You are likely used to quickly tossing a few keywords into a search bar to get background information on topics with which you aren't very familiar. As the web comic XKCD put it in a flowchart on becoming "the local computer expert": "Google the name of the [software] plus a few words related to what you want to do. Follow any instructions."[6] (See figure 1.2.) The same rules apply here.

Practice Empathy

We think one of the best pieces of writing on technology training remains Phil Agre's 1996 essay "How to Help Someone Use a Computer."[7] Agre reminds us that none of us were born knowing how to use computers, no matter how *born digital* we might be. He offers an often-forgotten reason why people learning about tech can easily get frustrated or impatient: "A computer is a means to an end. The person you're helping probably cares mostly about the end. This is reasonable." And, maybe most important of all, he points out the underlying problems with the experience of using many technologies: "Whenever [people] start to blame themselves, respond by blaming the computer. Then keep on blaming the computer, no matter how many times it takes, in a calm, authoritative tone of voice." Think about when you've seen patrons attempting to navigate the disjointed maze that is finding, borrowing, and accessing e-books or journal articles. They might take it out on themselves, blaming their lack of tech abilities, but no, that mess is all ours—or, well, our vendors'.

Be Approachable

Another key part of providing good reference service is approachability, and in a technology-oriented sense, this includes the channels through which patrons can approach you. You should give them as many channels as you can, not only through the traditional ones of coming up to a desk in person or setting up a one-on-one, but by offering e-mail and chat reference services too. In chapter 4, we talk about communication between members of library IT (information technology) teams and how online ticketing systems facilitate online reference services; they often also include phone numbers to which patrons can text their questions. Another advantage of ticketing systems is the ease with which they help keep track of the kinds of questions being asked; they make it possible to generate a list of frequently asked questions (FAQs) that actually get asked—versus the FAQs we see all too often that read like lists of questions librarians *wish* their patrons would ask.

Social media platforms can also provide a way to engage with people, though we'd recommend using them mostly as a way of setting up a time to talk in another setting. Similarly, you can offer to continue chats or e-mail conversations in person or over the phone if a question might be better answered that way, offer one-on-one appointments, or mention upcoming workshops. Though it ultimately comes down to a patron's preference and comfort level, tech troubleshooting can be much more effective and less abstract when both parties are looking at the same screen.

NOISE, PHONES, AND FOOD

Libraries are no longer places for silent study; we removed *shushing* from our job descriptions long ago. Cell phones as well as food and drink in the library are changing library culture very quickly. These concerns probably have the most impact on public libraries, though all types of libraries are seeing and responding to them.

Today's library patrons are not just comparing your library to other libraries, but also to Starbucks and Barnes & Noble, as well as their own living rooms. While there is a significant number of users who want and expect the traditional library environment (quiet, calm, that "book smell"), many others are looking for a place they can be comfortable in, sometimes for long periods of time. This means having easy access to power for charging devices, communicating via text and voice calls, and sipping their favorite caffeine-laden beverage. Some patrons want quiet, but others are looking to plug in to a new kind of social interaction: being alone together. Still others want to interact and collaborate and don't want to be quiet at all.

How can staff manage patron expectations in a busy, active environment? How can we accommodate all these behaviors along with differences in age and demographics? How can we compete with Starbucks and the like if we set extreme time limits, don't allow phone calls, or don't let people have their lattes?

One way is through zoning. Different areas of the building can be designated as active, silent, or in-between. Many libraries are allowing covered beverages throughout the building (with the exception of historical rooms or rare collection areas), and we encourage this. Food can be allowed in some areas (such as teen rooms and café spaces) and not others.

An efficient way to organize zoning in the library is to make the area immediately inside the entrance the most active and permissive area and then become progressively restrictive moving into the building. Many academic libraries and large public libraries configure zoning by floor, with the lowest level being the most active space and the top level as silent study space. If your library is only one floor and/or very small, zoning can work to some extent, but it's very important to provide at least one enclosed, acoustically separated space for those who want quiet—even with excellent acoustical engineering design, sound will carry.

If you don't already have policies around these issues (or if your policies are traditional and restrictive, banning all beverages and cell phone use), your staff and governing body should review different approaches and consider which could work in your library. It's essential that we be prepared to evolve along with patron expectations; the way people are using our buildings is changing, and we must change with them.

NOTES

1. Retail Customer Service, "Generation Gap Narrowing When It Comes to Customer Service," May 14, 2015, www.retailcustomerexperience.com/news/generation-gap-narrowing-when-it-comes-to-customer-service/.
2. Stelios Tsafarakis, Theodosios Kokotas, and Angelos Pantouvakis, "A Multiple Criteria Approach for Airline Passenger Satisfaction Measurement and Service Quality Improvement," *Journal of Air Transport Management* 68 (May 2018): 61–75, https://doi.org/10.1016/j.jairtraman.2017.09.010.

3. Feng Hu et al., "Evolving Customer Expectations of Hospitality Services: Differences in Attribute Effects on Satisfaction and Re-patronage," *Tourism Management* 74 (October 2019): 345–57, https://doi.org/10.1016/j.tourman .2019.04.010.

4. MacRumors, "Apple Stores," May 12, 2020, www.macrumors.com/roundup/ apple-retail-stores/.

5. American Library Association, "Number of Libraries in the United States: Home," June 14, 2019, https://libguides.ala.org/numberoflibraries.

6. XKCD.com, "XKCD Comic #627," August 4, 2012, www.explainxkcd.com/wiki/ index.php/File:tech_support_cheat_sheet.png.

7. Phil Agre, "How to Help Someone Use a Computer," 1996, https://pages.gseis .ucla.edu/faculty/agre/how-to-help.html.

2
Users at the Center of Everything

Librarians have been applying user experience (UX) principles to library services for many years, but it's not yet universal practice. The term *user experience* has roots in technology, specifically in terms of how humans interact with machines. While there's no definitive creator of the concept, Don Norman, author of *The Design of Everyday Things* and former consultant to Apple, was among the first people to talk about the usability and enjoyability, or lack thereof, of human-computer interaction during the early days of personal computing.[1] Technology companies of today have whole UX departments and teams devoted to evaluating and reevaluating the myriad aspects of the products or services they put out into the world.

Similarly, you might say Aaron Schmidt and Amanda Etches, coauthors of *Useful, Usable, Desirable: A Librarian's Guide to User Experience Design*, opened the library world's eyes to the importance of the three interwoven components in the title.[2] For good UX, a product or service must be useful, usable, *and* desirable. Many libraries have followed the lead and hired dedicated UX folks or listed UX skills as an aspect or a responsibility in reference job descriptions. Such positions often come with a technology focus, though we've met UX librarians who tackle all the other service points a patron encounters in addition to tech.

In this chapter, we talk about the basics of library UX design, starting with library technology and the challenges and opportunities it presents and then addressing the incorporation of these principles into the physical environment. Finally, we discuss the UX skills that we feel should be cultivated by just about every staff person in a library. We have no objection to hiring a dedicated UX coordinator, but frontline staff and administrators should be encouraged to adopt the same practices and mind-sets.

CRASH COURSE IN UX

A common misperception is that you need a lot of time and money to embark on a program of integrating UX ideas into your library—far from it. The key is to shift your thinking and consider every aspect of service from the user's point of view. Everything from your voice mail message to your policy manual plays a part.

First, Some Jargon

User experience design is the philosophy of considering spaces, services, and processes from the end user's point of view. The term originated in the digital world in the field of human-machine interaction, was picked up by product designers, and, from there, has filtered into every aspect of life, including the library.

Human-centered design began in the fields of ergonomics and accessibility and is now nearly synonymous with UX design, at least in this context.

Design thinking means looking at a process or project with a fresh perspective, an approach that can change the outcome dramatically. If your process isn't getting results, a simple design-thinking exercise can get your creative juices flowing.

You can put these ideas into practice incrementally, starting with tiny changes and building up to larger, system-wide innovations. The concept at the core of the whole UX movement is empathy. Learning to look at a situation with a beginner's mind—putting aside all your years of education and experience in librarianship and seeing your library from a new user's point of view—is the key. Realistically, most people who walk into the building aren't familiar with your procedures and policies, your cataloging and classification systems, the building layout, or the incredible range of services you offer. How can your physical space be changed, even slightly, to help them understand the library?

Empathy is about meeting people where they are rather than where you think they should be. The goal is to make the experience as intuitive and easy as possible; to give users visual clues that help them navigate their way and accomplish their goals. Many librarians rail against old stereotypes, yet we continue to perpetuate them by maintaining barriers, both physical and psychological, between staff and patrons.

CELEBRATION OF FAILURE

In her professional life, Lauren has worked for three architectural firms, one zoo, one multinational corporation, two museums, five universities, three public libraries, and one state library agency. She has also done freelance work or consulting in both architecture and librarianship. Over thirty-two years she has worked in ten US states, three Canadian provinces, and one eastern European country. That's a lot of opportunity for failure.

Lauren came from a white, upper-middle-class background, where the understood goal in life was to be professionally successful. Go to college, get a degree or two (or three), get a good job (or twelve). Work hard. Be successful. So how does failure figure into this scenario?

For a long time, failure was completely unacceptable. Lauren is in her early sixties now and still remembers the crushing defeat when she received her first C in ninth-grade algebra. She's done pretty well at pleasing most of her employers, but not all. And it's been only in the past several years that she's begun seeing and truly understanding the value of those failures.

Maybe it's more accurate to say that she's changed her understanding of the word *failure*. Lauren used to think success was getting the right answer, getting a good grade, achieving the correct outcome. What she didn't see was that in order to do this, the result had to be predetermined. There was no room for deviation from the known course of action.

Opening her mind to other possibilities gave her the freedom to try new ways of thinking, achieving unexpected results. Eureka! Trial and error has been part of the scientific method for centuries, but for many years, Lauren was focused on the right answer rather than the unexpected one.

Wrong answers lead to breakthroughs in every part of life, if we can embrace and then learn from them. This is true on levels both macro (being fired) and micro (making a mistake when typing this sentence). Accepting that mistakes are not a bad thing leads to more experimentation and some really great ideas. "Fail fast and fail often" is a well-known motto—just Google it for a myriad of business articles on the topic.

SERVICE DESIGN

Most librarians are committed to public service and know what that means, but we love definitions. According to Merriam-Webster, *service* is

2 a : the work performed by one that serves <good -> **b :** HELP, USE, BENEFIT <glad to be of -> **c :** contribution to the welfare of others

On the other hand, a lot of people are afraid of the word *design*. They don't think of themselves as designers. However, *design* is

5 . . . **b :** a plan or protocol for carrying out or accomplishing something . . . ; *also* : the process of preparing this[3]

Not so scary, right? And when we combine these, we get this:

Service design is a plan or protocol for carrying out or accomplishing a contribution to the welfare of others.

Service is what libraries do. The shift from library as repository to library as provider of information and experience is a given. Service design is how we do that.

Overall Service Philosophy

What is a welcoming place? A place where you want to spend time; a place where you can relax; a place that invites you to put your feet on the furniture. Think about what makes you feel comfortable and incorporate that spirit into your library. This is how you create a culture of excellent customer service.

Make sure these concepts are written down, formally adopted as part of your strategic planning, and reinforced through ongoing training. They must be a high priority for everyone from frontline staff to the director. They must also be applied consistently across the board, from the visiting city council member to the person who is experiencing homelessness.

Policies

The strategic plan lays out the foundational concepts and philosophy of the library, and the official written policies detail the ways these ideas will be carried out. If you haven't reviewed your policy manual for a while, do it now. How many of those policies were developed with the user's experience in mind, and how many reflect the "That's how we've always done it" attitude? Which ones place tradition and staff preference above excellent customer service?

One of the "15 Action Steps for Library Leaders" in *Rising to the Challenge: Re-envisioning Public Libraries*, from the Aspen Institute, is this: "Change long-held rules and operating procedures that impede the development of the library's spaces and platform."[4]

What, for your library, is etched in stone? Should it be?

Strategic Plans

When Lauren was a new library director, she thought of the strategic planning process as a necessary evil. The plan was something she was required to do— one of those bureaucratic hoops that we all have to jump through. It wasn't until years later when she realized that the strategic plan is an essential tool that guides not only policy making and big decisions but the everyday operations of the library. The plan should be a living, working document, and yearly action plans should build on the strategic plan with specific goals for each year.

There are many styles and methods for developing and writing a strategic plan, well documented in other sources. The best plans are short, concise, and to the point. Long narratives waste the time of the reader and confuse the issue. It's better to take the time to condense the concepts into bullet points, lists, and short statements of goals and objectives. These are more useful, and good graphic design makes the information quickly and easily grasped.

> "I have made this letter longer than usual, only because I have not had the time to make it shorter."
>
> **—BLAISE PASCAL**

FIGURE 2.1
The Cary Memorial Library uses powerful, emotional language to drive its mission and define its core values. Strategic priorities like "A Place That Works for Everyone" inspire concrete plans for action, clear commitments to the philosophy articulated by the library's mission and values, and ample room for flexibility and improvement ("We are a work in progress").

A PLACE THAT WORKS FOR EVERYONE

We value the rich diversity of our community, and our commitment to equitable service for all is unwavering. Efforts to identify and remove barriers to access are ongoing — we are a work in progress.

- Our spaces, collections, programs, and exhibits present unique opportunities to showcase different voices and experiences. We collaborate extensively with individuals and groups interested in leveraging library resources. We support and amplify the work of community partners who share our mission and values.

- Community voices are essential in our efforts to make Cary Library a truly inclusive, diverse, equitable, and accessible place. We are asking questions, listening attentively, and working hard to make meaningful changes.

- We want the community to see their own diversity reflected in the library staff. To that end, we will continue to build a diverse team of individuals who are constantly strengthening their cultural competency and societal awareness.

One of the best recent examples of a strategic plan we've seen is from the Cary Memorial Library in Lexington, Massachusetts (see figure 2.1).[5] It's clean, it's clear, and it's easily readable. Staff members at all levels of responsibility can use this document to help them understand how their work fits in with the larger goals of the institution, building consistency, and morale.

If your building has physical or functionality issues or services that you'd like to provide aren't currently possible (for whatever reason), make sure these are listed in the strategic plan and the yearly action plans. A well-crafted plan is a powerful tool for change.

Trustees or other governing bodies are crucial to the success (or failure) of the plan. They should be instrumental in developing the plan and must have a significant level of buy-in for things to happen. If you have trustees who are resistant to change or chronic naysayers, suggest that they become a librarian for a day, shadowing you and/or a frontline worker to see what really goes on in the library and why you are proposing certain initiatives. It may open their eyes.

Brand Identity

One of the key aspects to good service design is a comprehensive program of brand identity and visual reinforcement of that identity. Every communication should be identifiable as coming from your library. As we mentioned in the introduction, we adapted our book's organizational structure from Patience and Fortitude, the stone lions that have become the recognized logo of the New York Public Library. Their image is used and visible everywhere in the library's branding. (See figure 2.2.) Your library may not have as striking a symbol, but try to think of some icon you could use—a prominent tree, the local school's mascot, a riff on your library's name, or something related to the town or community where your library is located. If your institution is large, you may have a visual identity manual, including guidelines for use of colors, logos, tone of voice, and so on. If you don't have such a manual, create one! It doesn't have to be long or complex. The important thing is that you make conscious choices and maintain consistency.[6]

FIGURE 2.2
The New York Public Library's lion logo is truly iconic (and inspired the design motif of this book).

Do People Recognize the Library's Brand?

Everything associated with the library should be immediately recognizable through the consistent use of the library's official logo as well as coordinating typefaces and colors. Review everything and make sure the staff understand the reasons for doing this.

Physical Objects

- signage: exterior and interior
- print: brochures, flyers, publications (and get rid of handwritten paper signs taped up everywhere!)

Digital Presence

- website
- apps
- digital signage

Reuse/repost content in multiple places and formats. It's okay if somebody sees the same communication from you on Instagram and Facebook as well as the same information on flyers and digital signage. Many people will come to you only in person or only on your website or only on social media, and so forth. Meet your users (and nonusers) where they are and be intentional about your library's representation in your communications.

Improving the Library Experience

How can you smooth the service experience at your library? What could be done to make services more transparent? If patrons approach a service desk and ask for help, how do you think they feel if the staff member says, "We can't do that here; you have to go to X desk on Y floor," or recommends that they talk to someone who isn't in at the moment, or suggests some other convoluted process? To your users, everyone who works in a library is a librarian. It's not our job to educate them on the merits of an advanced degree in library science; it's our job to help them find what they need. Don't make people learn your organizational chart; they don't care. The default answer to every "Can you help me?" question should be "Yes," or at least "Let's see what we can do for you." Staff must engage with every person in front of them and learn to read the patrons. Ask if they want you to teach them how to search for something or if they just want you to find what they're seeking for them. Tailoring services to the individual and not the lowest common denominator is a learned skill, and staff training can transform the ways your employees interact with users.

Touchpoints

The principles we're talking about can be applied at every scale, from the 10,000-foot view to the tiny details. It's very easy to become overwhelmed when thinking about changing your library to incorporate UX principles. Don't panic, though—you can start small. UX plays a part in every conceivable interaction between the user and your library. From a flyer about programs to the library's smartphone app to the broken lock on the partition in your restrooms—all of these impact user experience. Your online presence plays a part as well—from your website to social media platforms and mobile apps.

Think about what patrons hear when they call your library on the telephone. Does a human answer with a pleasant welcome? If this isn't the case, must they navigate a complicated (and often frustrating) automated system? Are they forced to wait through a long message with hours and location information before they get to an opportunity to connect with a department or an extension?

What about the community notice board? Is it messy and filled with flyers that expired months (or years) ago? Is a staff member or reliable volunteer assigned to monitor it? Do you have enough space? Are library notices separated from community information?

And what about those library flyers and brochures? Are they well designed, with a uniform look and recognizable branding? A professional graphic designer is great to have on staff, but most libraries don't have that luxury. Basic design principles can be employed to make the pieces look good, regardless of who produces them.

Points of Contact between the Library and Its Users, aka *Touchpoints*

- website
- integrated library system (ILS)
- databases
- e-mail
- instant/text messaging
- online reference help
- telephone and voice mail
- parking lot
- building
- signage
- furniture and shelving
- computer rooms and equipment
- service desks (circulation and reference)
- collections
- programs/events
- brochures/flyers/business cards
- newsletters/advertising
- staff training
- social media

Adapted from Aaron Schmidt and Amanda Etches, *Useful, Usable, Desirable: Applying User Experience Design to Your Library* (Chicago: ALA Editions, 2014), 2.

Above all, approach every interaction in a positive light if at all possible. Everyone has had bad experiences in shops, with customer service reps, in government offices, and, yes, even in libraries—we call it the Wall of No. When you ask a question and the first response is negative, it's a total turnoff and the memory of the interaction is unpleasant, regardless of the ultimate outcome. If you can't answer yes to a question, try "Let me see what we can do for you" or something similar. Model this behavior and teach your staff, from shelvers to management, to do the same.

Consider every interaction your patrons have with the library, from a program flyer in a drugstore window to a complex reference transaction. With each step in the process, learn how to minimize pain points and maximize customer satisfaction.

As an example, here's a trick for defusing a phone call with an unhappy patron that Callan learned while working at a public library. She asked for the patron's name and pulled up their borrower record while listening to them express their disappointment that the day before, the library hadn't remembered to record a phone message to alert people to a holiday closure. Though Callan couldn't undo the mistake, with the patron's record opened, she could see that they had a book checked out that was about to be due. After apologetically listening and promising to do better next time, Callan asked the patron if they'd like to renew the book. The patron was delighted to be asked about it and happily said yes. It wasn't a huge gesture, but it helped Callan end the call with a bit more goodwill on both ends of the phone.

Design Thinking

Design thinking and human-centered design are two different ways to approach the same basic concept: how to get out of your own head and into your users'. The idea is to use techniques to help shift the human brain out of familiar ways of thinking and generate creative solutions. The end goal is always to foster empathy and see things from a different perspective, usually that of the user or service consumer. In this way, design thinking is a great way to enhance your library's UX philosophy.

As an architect and a librarian, Lauren finds that many people don't consider themselves to be designers or creative in any way. In actuality, we are all designers simply by living our lives—what we choose to wear, how we arrange our homes and workspaces (or don't), which books we read, and the TV shows we watch (or don't). These are all design decisions. You are the designer of your life, whether you do it consciously or not. Through spreadsheets, oil paints, words, or singing in the shower, we are all creative. The maker movement is just the newest recognition of the human need to express ourselves.

Design thinking is a creative approach, or a series of steps, that will help you design meaningful solutions for your library. It's also a mind-set, because you start to think like a designer, even if you don't consider yourself one.

Any kind of service can be transformed and made better. Let's take one example: the core service of identifying, finding, and checking out a book. How do your users identify an item they want to borrow?

- word-of-mouth recommendation
- school booklist
- social media post or ad
- browsing
- readers' advisory service
- online catalog search

Imagine each of these possibilities from the patron's *and* the staff's point of view. Use personas (more on this later) and think about what the customer wants. Are they a grab-it-and-go kind of person? Or do they want to talk to a staff member and seek personalized service? Do they need an in-depth reference interview to determine what they're really looking for? Are they a digital native who likes chat-based reference, or do they want to get up close and personal?

Once the item is located, what checkout options are available? Is your e-book and e-audio service user-friendly? Can a person in a hurry grab their DVD from the hold shelf, use the nearby self-checkout station, and be on their way? What happens when the book they want isn't on the shelf or isn't in the collection at all?

All of these scenarios require a different approach and series of steps to implement. In public libraries, we are blessed and cursed with the full gamut of personalities, ages, and skill levels. The ability to read a patron and tailor services to that patron's needs is not something most people are born with; it takes practice.

Here are a few simple places to start:

- Ask up front how much time the user has; this can help set the tone of the interaction.
- Ask the user if they want you to look up something for them, or show them how to use search techniques themselves.
- If the user wants a particular item or books on a specific subject, offer to walk them to the appropriate area in the shelves if at all possible.
- If self-checkout is a new service at the library, make sure a staff person is nearby at all times to help newbies through the process, and always offer at least one traditional staffed checkout station for those who prefer it.

Try to remember that most people using the library are not well-versed in classification systems and don't keep detailed knowledge of your materials and procedures in their heads. Things that you can do in your sleep are

FIGURE 2.3
Post-it notes and markers for quick idea generation and recording are standard tools of the trade for design thinking.

brand-new and confusing concepts to many. The point is to make collections and services accessible.

Describing in words how a design-thinking process or exercise works is tough. There's almost always a magic moment during the process when everyone looks around with that "Eureka!" sparkle in their eyes. The process is experiential, iterative, and a lot of fun. It facilitates suspension of judgment, rampant brainstorming, and the generation of wild moonshot ideas. It requires stepping out of your comfort zone, though, and can feel chaotic and raw.

It's important to understand that design thinking is not a discrete series of steps, and there's no easy checklist that you can go through and be done. This is a mind-set shift that, if you commit to it, will change the way you see the world.

One tool we've found to help with this shift in thinking is IDEO's design toolkit. IDEO's website provides a wealth of ideas, developed specifically for libraries, on how to get started.[7] The website has an array of tools, resources, and exercises that you can use, including "How might we . . . ?" statements, personas, and rapid prototyping. We've also written our own UX guide for librarians that includes a slide deck we use in our workshops as well as a targeted series of blurbs, videos, and exercises.[8]

The only way to truly understand design thinking is to jump in with both feet. Grab some Post-its and Sharpies and give it a go. (See figure 2.3.) Remember the tenet "Fail early and often"—that's the only way to learn.

Trends in User Experience Design

The world of personal and business computing was all about voice-controlled devices and assistants in 2019 before virtual meeting software transformed the way we worked and socialized during the COVID-19 pandemic. Machines are being taught how to classify images, identify objects, and drive taxis. The CRISPR gene alteration tool sits at the brink of potentially revolutionizing medicine, and we're sending reusable rockets into space. Cars and buildings are being 3-D printed. Still, researchers marvel at the fact that what seems most crucial for continued loyalty to a company, store, or brand is the perceived quality of customer service.

"E-customers' loyalty to a specific service or app no longer results merely from adequate functionality, decent usability and aesthetic look of an app," write the authors of a 2017 paper about emerging trends in human-computer interaction.[9] "Now it primarily results from cumulated, constantly positive user experience." What makes for that "cumulated, constantly positive" experience? Some researchers would tell you it's all about trust. Trust is a hard thing to measure, but we found a fascinating study that correlates usability and appearance with trust levels on news websites.[10] The authors discuss a methodology in human-computer interaction called Attracdiff, which uses a number of "bipolar verbal anchors" to help test users describe their gut reactions to interfaces. They're essentially antonym combinations, like "gaudy–classy," "amateurish–professional," and "ugly–beautiful." These in turn guide the design of user interfaces with aspects called *hedonic qualities* that "appeal to a person's desire of pleasure and avoidance of boredom and discomfort."[11]

Claudio Pinhanez, writing from IBM's T. J. Watson Research Center, describes it this way: "Dealing with an online service provider always involves an exchange of trust between the parties."[12] He goes on to make a comparison between restaurants and apps, suggesting that places where the kitchen is open and visible aren't so very different from food delivery and ride hailing apps that show you exactly where your driver is. "Increasing the visibility of back-office operations in traditional services often improves also service quality," Pinhanez writes.

How does that apply to library technology? We can and should be demanding better interfaces from our technology vendors, both for the sake of our staff's sanity and our patrons' time. In the meantime, we can be more transparent and honest about the clunkiness of using our technology and platforms. That might seem unnecessarily self-deprecating, but it's not meant to be negative—we can better set expectations this way. Imagine all of those information literacy tutorials during which time was spent apologizing for the un-Googley-ness of your discovery service. While we wait and continue to advocate for usability improvements, it's important to tell people that they might encounter snags they're not used to seeing elsewhere.

The interesting question here, and the balance we should aspire to strike, is whether some of those snags *should* be part of the process. In *How to Do Nothing*, the artist/author Jenny Odell writes, "The experience of research is exactly opposite to the way I usually often encounter information online. When you research a subject, you make a series of important decisions, not least what it is you want to research."[13] Compare that to mindlessly scrolling through a social news feed or looking at only the Wikipedia blurb on the top or right side of a search results page, an activity that is meant to be as effortless as can be. "You make a commitment to spend time finding information that doesn't immediately present itself," Odell goes on to say about research. "You select different sources that you understand may be biased for various reasons." The challenge here is that Google has figured out how to make people think they're finding *all* of the information out there about a given topic, regardless of whether that's true and regardless of the biases and commercial processes that influence search behavior. Though we'd like to think that most folks would tell you they trust their local library more than they trust Google, we're guessing they're not turning to the library's search bar for the vast majority of their queries. Something else is at play in the way muscle memory kicks in when you type "google .com" or hit CTRL+T to open a new tab and start a new search.

As far as building trust through physical transparency, there's plenty about what librarians and libraries do that's invisible to the public. In some research libraries even today, stacks are closed and only those trained in the arcane art of librarianship are allowed to enter the sacred halls. In the early twentieth century, the concept of open stacks resulted in fortuitous browsing—finding related materials on the shelf next to the item the patron was seeking—enhancing the user experience. So how can we do better with opening ourselves up?

Placing a window to allow the public to view the automated materials handling (AMH) machine might be flashier than highlighting the human worker scanning in books at the returns workstation, but both demystify the process and start to educate patrons in all the work that goes on backstage. One library near us in Massachusetts provides occasional behind-the-scenes library tours during which they bring patrons into staff areas so they can see cataloging and processing in action and watch their AMH machine do its magic sorting into bins. This is a double win: it humanizes and validates library staff while also building trust in the library's process.

NEEDS ASSESSMENT AND PLANNING

Before launching into creating solutions, you have to know exactly what the problem is. As in the reference interview, you have to dig into every situation at the start and make sure you're asking the right questions—keep going until you find the nub. Assessing your needs comes first, and coming up with a plan of attack follows.

Identifying the User

One of the critical steps in the UX process is identifying who your users are. Depending on the type of library you work in, these groups might apply:

patrons (or customers or whatever you call them), students, faculty, nonresidents, and staff.

Each of these groups can be broken down further. For example, in an academic library, you might have undergraduate students and graduate students or students from different colleges or disciplines. Staff will encompass professional and support staff or union and exempt or faculty and nonfaculty. Patrons in public libraries are wildly diverse: seniors and adults; young adults, teens, and tweens; children and preschoolers; new residents; early readers; people with disabilities; and more. Lauren worked for more than twenty years in public libraries in resort towns with special patron categories such as second homeowners and seasonal workers. Every one of these groups has differing and sometimes competing needs and preferences.

Personas (Breaking It Down)

One tool that can be of enormous help in defining your users is the persona. A persona is a representation of a major user group in your library. You'll have to

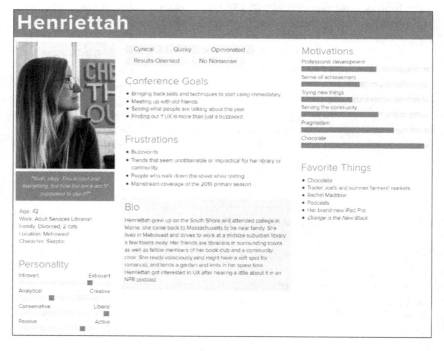

FIGURE 2.4
This persona, a fictional librarian working outside Boston, was created with a tool called Xtensio (https://xtensio.com) to help Callan and Lauren guide the design of a talk they presented on user experience at a Massachusetts library conference.

develop several personas in order to capture the majority of users, and some patrons will fit more than one persona. The goal is to create a deep and rounded understanding of the user, drawing on and deepening empathy. (See figure 2.4.) When developing personas, you can use in-depth interviews and focus groups to get a better handle on the details rather than making assumptions.

You may think you already know your users—sometimes too well—but it's worth your time to consider what you don't know and dig a little deeper. You will likely be surprised at what you find.

Assessing Community Needs

Before you can effect positive change, it's important to assess where you are and what you need. What services might you provide if you had more money, resources, or space?

Common sense makes the community you serve the best starting point for developing any public amenity, including libraries. The Project for Public Spaces is an organization that enumerates eleven core principles for analyzing and creating physical places that foster community.[14]

Wherever you are, there are people who can provide a historical perspective, valuable insights into how the area functions, and an understanding of the critical issues and what is meaningful to people in the community. Tapping this information at the beginning of the process will help to create a sense of community ownership in the project that can be of great benefit to both the library and the community.

As part of your library's strategic plan (and, yes, you really do need one of these), you need to gather opinions and information from the public regarding their preferences and desires for service, as well as your local context. Don't limit yourself to just that, though; most library patrons (and especially people who don't use the library at all) are not aware of forward-thinking ideas in the library field. Do some research to find out what's going on in other libraries, either in your area or far afield. If you're like us, every trip, whether for business or pleasure, is an opportunity to investigate new libraries and see what their facilities and services are like. Are they doing something successful that you might copy? Most librarians are eager to share their experiences and ideas, so feel free to ask questions.

START SMALL, THINK BIG

This way of working is not easy for many people. It requires, for most of us, a major mind-set shift in which we embrace uncertainty, look at situations with a beginner's mind, accept a constant state of incompletion, and allow ourselves (and others) to fail. Remember that we are all designers, whether we know it or not, and we can step outside of our comfort zones to make our libraries better.

Simple incremental steps go a long way toward effecting change. Start with a new voice mail message or venture out from behind the desk to help patrons on the floor. Try something new. If it doesn't work, try something else. There are no mistakes!

Continuous Gradual Improvement: Tackle the Low-Hanging Fruit First

It's weird to think about the timelessness of libraries. They can *just exist* in a way that other types of institutions and businesses can't because *the library* is a concept as well as a collection and a building. Libraries don't *have* to try to grow or change in any particular way to please their stakeholders—at least not in a way that is concretely governed by measures like profits in a given quarter. Similarly, the standards we use to evaluate the quality of our libraries are not universal, as they might be in public or higher education. This is why we say you need a strategic plan: you have to define your own standards of quality and goals.

In the absence of such a plan, or if a plan is outdated or ignored, libraries tend to just . . . stop. Best case, this means they're functioning well enough but aren't expanding their services or evaluating what they're missing. Worst case, it means they're not functioning on one or more important levels. Strategic plans aren't a cure-all, but if they're done from a user-centered perspective (like the plan from Cary Memorial Library described in chapter 2), they are a way to dig into both what's not working and what the community wants and needs. By asking the right questions, you can find both big and small things that need attention. In turn, you can start by fixing the small problems, then you can contend with the medium-sized ones, and then start putting the bigger ones on a schedule. As you go along, toss aside any suggestions that don't fit or save them to reevaluate later.

MAKE THINGS INTUITIVE AND EASY

Steve Krug's renowned web design book *Don't Make Me Think* is all about the importance of usability and findability in the digital world.[15] These qualities are just as valid in physical environments—how many times have you seen patrons walk in the library entrance and then stop to gaze around with a lost look on their faces? Think about ways to help people navigate their world. Remove clutter and work toward providing clear and consistent visual, auditory, and tactile cues.

Meet people where they are, not where you think they should be. Tear down the Wall of No and listen to what people really need. Librarians are great at the reference interview—shift that technique a bit and use it in every single interaction. Each interaction doesn't have to be perfect or long. Tweak your approach to accommodate the person in front of you, who is sure to appreciate the personal service.

Following traditional ways of operating, dictated by huge policy manuals and complicated procedures, serves only to reinforce the old-fashioned stereotype of librarians in buns. We're not advocating anarchy, but libraries are no longer the only game in town, so we have to make our libraries comfortable and responsive—places where people want to go to spend time.

NOTES

1. Don Norman, *The Design of Everyday Things* (New York: Basic Books, 2013).
2. Aaron Schmidt and Amanda Etches, *Useful, Usable, Desirable: Applying User Experience Design to your Library* (Chicago: ALA Editions, 2014).
3. *Merriam-Webster's Collegiate Dictionary*, 11th ed. (Springfield, MA: Merriam-Webster, 2003), 1137 and 338, respectively.
4. Amy K. Garmer, *Rising to the Challenge: Re-envisioning Public Libraries* (Washington, DC: The Aspen Institute, 2014), 50, https://csreports.aspen institute.org/dialogue-on-public-libraries/2014/report.
5. Cary Memorial Library, "Our Guiding Principles," www.carylibrary.org/sites/default/files/CMLGuidingPrinciples.pdf.
6. MilesHerndon, "Branding 101: A Visual Brand Identity Checklist," MilesHerndon.com blog, November 16, 2015, https://milesherndon.com/blog/branding-101-visual-brand-identity/.
7. IDEO, "Design Thinking for Libraries," https://designthinkingforlibraries.com.
8. Callan Bignoli and Lauren Stara, "Elements of UX: A Librarian's Guide to User Experience Design," http://guides.mblc.state.ma.us/elements-of-ux.
9. Krzysztof Marasek, Andrzej Romanowski, and Marcin Sikorski, "Emerging Trends and Novel Approaches in Interaction Design" (paper presented at FedCSIS, the Federated Conference on Computer Science and Information Systems, Prague, Czech Republic, September 3–6, 2017), https://annals-csis.org/proceedings/2017/drp/005.html.
10. Jaigris Hodson and Brian Traynor, "Design Exploration of Fake News: A Transdisciplinary Methodological Approach to Understanding Content Sharing and Trust on Social Media" (paper presented at ProComm, the IEEE International Professional Communication Conference, Toronto, ON, July 22–25, 2018), https://ieeexplore.ieee.org/document/8476675.
11. Usability First, "Glossary: Hedonic Quality," www.usabilityfirst.com/glossary/hedonic-quality/.
12. Claudio Pinhanez, "A Service Science Perspective on Human-Computer Interface Issues of Online Service Applications," *International Journal of Information Systems in the Service Sector* 1, no. 2 (April–June 2009): 25, http://pinhanez.com/claudio/publications/ijisss09.pdf.
13. Jenny Odell, *How to Do Nothing* (Brooklyn, NY: Melville House, 2019), 175.
14. Project for Public Spaces, "Eleven Principles for Creating Great Community Places," www.pps.org/reference/11steps.
15. Steve Krug, *Don't Make Me Think* (San Francisco: New Riders, 2005).

PART II
Patience

Rome wasn't built in a day, and your flexible, creative, change-friendly library won't be either. We've got some advice for tackling both the large-scale philosophical shifts and the concrete tasks that lie ahead. Strap yourself in; it can take a while before it feels like you're making any progress, but with some patience you will start to see a shift. Each tiny, incremental step contributes to the whole and can eventually lead to fundamental change.

3

Leading the Way in the Face of Change

What is leadership? In our view, a leader is someone who can use their passion to effect change and stir others to feel that same passion and get excited about the change. If you are in library management or administration, we invite you to think about the difference between being a manager and being a leader. We know plenty of people at the top of organizations who are good managers but not-so-great leaders. The library profession needs to do a better job of fostering and welcoming leadership, and not just at the top of the pyramid. Anyone at any level should be empowered to lead and effect change.

FOSTERING A CHANGE-FRIENDLY WORK CULTURE

A new project of any scope can feel daunting. Many library staff members are already overwhelmed with day-to-day tasks, and the idea of taking on any additional planning work can feel impossible. Remember that even tiny, incremental change can have a huge impact. Encourage staff at all levels to contribute to the assessment and design of your service model. No idea is bad; some may be difficult and ultimately unworkable, but others that seem wild at first can turn into a breakthrough in customer service. Building trust to foster change means withholding judgment and giving all input sincere consideration.

Callan likes to say, "I'm a librarian. I give the benefit of the doubt to people for a living." As librarians, we have to do this to be in our business; we have to assume the best in people to be able to let them borrow our things, and for the most part we're able to rely on that trust. How can we leverage that assumption to help members of our profession overcome a resistance to change? What is it about the nature of checking out an item to patrons that transcends the automatic tendency to expect the worst? What does this say about whether library staff members *actually are* resistant to change? Do they *really* expect the worst?

Some people, no matter what field they work in, are uncomfortable with change and do innately expect the worst. You'll encounter people like that just as often as you'll find people who are eager to throw out everything and start again, and along the way, you'll meet plenty of people who don't much care one way or the other. In our experience in Libraryland, the people who expect the worst can be of any age. They can work in any department and can have any color of hair from blonde to blue. The reasons for why they might feel the way they do about change are different from one person to the next. Some might be hesitant after previous work experiences. Some might be content with the workload they have and are wary about taking on more. Some of them might have perspectives you don't share or a vantage point you've never spent time in yourself. Some of them might just be jerks. But even the jerks can have legitimate points.

If you have staff members who are consistently unhappy or uncomfortable with change, it's important to treat them with respect and work to get at the reasons why. It's not a good idea to let them get away with not participating in meetings and exercises; they are entitled to their opinions but must explain them. They may shed important light on an issue that you haven't considered, thereby contributing to the conversation. This in turn gives them agency and shows them that their views are just as important as everyone else's. In this way, the most disruptive elements can become great assets.

Likewise, your staff—that means not just you—should be engaging your patrons, student body, or other user base as a critical piece of the change process. Community engagement and input are essential to every initiative. Why spend time, money, and effort on a great new program only to find out that nobody really wants it? If staff have a chance to see the true impetus for this change instead of just receiving orders from management, they will be more likely to embrace it. Make sure you and your staff have opportunities to consult your users often and in many different ways, and be transparent and responsive in your decision-making process.

What else can you do to get wary folks on board with change? You can learn a lot from what wasn't done well before you, as we advise in the following section about developing employee trust. Trust and change are intertwined. You can't expect people to get behind the changes you're making if they don't trust you. Communication is key and delegation is a necessity. Permission to be honest is crucial. Small acts build trust, and small changes build trust in bigger changes. Pace yourself and know when it's time to shelve projects. Give people a fair chance to guide change and express concerns, but don't leave yourself open to that feedback indefinitely. Be careful not to allow the negative voices to outweigh the positive ones. That last one is in direct defiance of human nature, and we know how hard it can be, but the fact of the matter is that you're not going to get everyone on your team in lockstep with your vision, just as your local library isn't going to have enough copies of the latest best seller on the shelf for everyone in town to borrow it the day it comes out.

A Note on Innovation

Steven Bell, in his 2019 article "Leading the Library That Leads the Way in Innovation," identifies three levels of innovation—incremental, evolutionary, and radical—and warns against innovation fatigue:

> Most library innovation is incremental, less risky, and likely to tweak what's working for better results. In addition to requiring less staff commitment, it often tackles unambiguous issues with clearly defined and limited change. Evolutionary change is a greater investment of time and effort, but staff comfortable with incremental change are likely ready for more challenging innovations. Radical innovation is rare. Since it requires a far greater commitment of time and resources, it should happen primarily when a significant opportunity presents itself and the library can establish a leadership role. In all cases, what library leaders bring to the table is their ability to influence colleagues to believe in and support innovation. It certainly helps to show that achieving the innovation would position the library as a leader within the organization or community.[*]

The word *innovation* itself is a fraught concept in librarianship and society as a whole. In her 2019 book *Race After Technology*, sociologist Ruha Benjamin quotes Andrew Russell and Lee Vinsel, who wrote that in order to "take the place of progress, 'innovation,' a smaller, and morally neutral, concept arose. Innovation provided a way to celebrate the accomplishments of a high-tech age without expecting . . . too much in the way of moral and social improvement."[*] We should think about how libraries also perpetuate innovation in this sense without an emphasis on moral and social improvement. In their 2018 *Library Trends* article, Isabel Espinal, Tonia Sutherland, and Charlotte Roh remind us, "We should not have to choose between technological focus and a diversity focus: both are future oriented and work well together."[‡]

* Steven Bell, "Leading the Library That Leads the Way in Innovation," *Library Journal*, October 24, 2019, www.libraryjournal.com/?detailStory=Leading-the-Library-That-Leads-the-Way-in-Innovation-Leading -from-the-Library.

† Cited in Ruha Benjamin, *Race After Technology* (Cambridge, UK: Polity, 2019), 79.

‡ Isabel Espinal, Tonia Sutherland, and Charlotte Roh, "A Holistic Approach for Inclusive Librarianship: Decentering Whiteness in Our Profession," *Library Trends* 67, no. 1 (2018): 158. https://muse.jhu.edu/ article/706993.

TRUST

Change is difficult. Human beings are hard-wired to prefer security, and constant change challenges that security at a fundamental level. "Fear of the unknown is deep-seated in the lizard brain," one librarian told us while we were writing this book. (See figure 3.1.) "We would rather not gain something better than give up what we have." For staff to feel safe in the midst of change, they must believe that they have agency in the process. When top-down, hierarchical organizations impose change on the staff, this leads to fear, anger, and poor morale. "I resist changes that are done to me, for me, in spite of me," another librarian said. "I am usually a reliable booster of change done with me, alongside me."

FIGURE 3.1
Even lizards need comfort sometimes.

Trust in the workplace is essential for a truly creative environment to flourish. A supportive and cooperative work environment involves all levels of staff in the decision-making process so that staff feel like they have at least a little control over the changes that are implemented. Employees take ownership of and are invested in the philosophy of the organization and the direction it is taking as a whole.

Most workplaces are neither all cooperative nor all authoritative, falling somewhere between these two extremes. Managing change and encouraging experimentation can be incredibly challenging. Most libraries and their parent organizations have a mix of enthusiastic innovators and old guard traditionalists. This book is not a treatise on personnel management—there are plenty of those out there. Our goal in this chapter is to help managers foster a culture of questioning and experimentation.

"A leader's job is to build and maintain trust, or, if needed, to restore it," we once heard a library director say. This is one of the important differences between a manager and a leader. It makes sense when you consider the challenges a new leader often confronts when starting a job, but before we follow that thread, let's define what we mean by trust in the workplace.

Trust is required when starting something new, whether that's making a small change to an existing service or launching a fresh strategic plan. It's necessary for morale and for getting the troops to follow the overarching organizational message. If you're in a leadership position, you need to take a prominent role in developing or redeveloping that message. To articulate the vision beyond your own mind, or the minds of your administrative team, you need the trust of people who will help move it past brainstorming and out into the world.

Trust is also knowing that constructive criticism will be heard and not dismissed or blown out of proportion. It's feeling like you can be vulnerable enough to talk to a manager about something that's making your job or personal life hard to the point where you need to say something about it. So much of trust has to do with communication, with balance, kindness, and, as social researcher Brené Brown tells us,[1] very small acts (remembering the name of a colleague's family member; making space for someone at the lunch table).

When you come into a job where you're tasked with making changes or you've been assigned a set of changes to make, whether you're in a leadership position or not, you're going to have to find a way to build or restore trust and then maintain it. For new employees, especially new managers, this can be a dicey task. Your predecessor may have left some serious baggage in their wake, something that might have seeded very real paranoia in the people who were around to endure it. Others may have tried the same thing you're attempting and failed at it. So how can you get people on your side, willing to suspend their disbelief?

As Brown would tell you, start small. Get to know everyone's names. Pay attention to the minute details of their lives. Do they have kids or elderly parents? Do they live locally? Do they have any hobbies or pets? From there, try to figure out what you can do to help people or at least make them feel heard. What is it that has upset them in the past? Unfairness or inconsistency (often in the form of favoritism)? Lack of communication or unclear expectations? Their own voices or opinions being ignored? Even if people aren't coming right out and telling you what's bothering them, they've likely experienced one or more of these problems in the past.

You can proactively respond to these common workplace trust breakers, not only by saying you'll do things differently, but—wait for it—*actually doing them differently*. Has the staff traditionally felt blindsided by sudden technology changes, like a rollout of new computer towers or printers? Let them know you're going to make the change, maybe by working with their department heads or asking them to help you create a plan together for the best time to do the work. Consider forming a cross-departmental technology committee to give updates to everyone in person and allow for pushback or alternative ideas, and make sure those committee members communicate with the rest of the staff. A key to effecting sustainable change and bringing people who trust you along for the ride is ensuring you're not coming off like a dictator, making decisions alone. This is also crucial for being able to delegate tasks that can be shared—not something you'll make any friends doing if you just bark out the orders without context, explanation, or encouragement. Delegation is something many new managers struggle with, but it can be an important trust builder, showing you have faith in others' ability to complete a task that might be new to them and demonstrating you'll be there as a resource for backup and help.

What do you do if you need to restore lost trust—either in you in particular or in the person (or people) who came before you in your position? First, let's talk about when it's you. It's time for some tough love. You're going to need to be blunt and honest about what went wrong. Increasingly, libraries have adopted a trend, with roots in big tech and business, to discuss failure in an open, constructive way, as we discussed in chapter 2. We think this is a good thing. Library conferences still have a tendency to focus on programs with positive outcomes, serving as a show-and-tell for when things went well. You don't hear much about missteps, but there's much to be learned when a project or plan goes off the rails.

When analyzing your own mistakes within the context of rebuilding workplace trust, you should start by thinking about your role in whatever went wrong. Break it down and be specific. Don't use passive voice or make it sound like the agency at play wasn't your own. Did you not communicate clearly? Did you think the desire would be much greater (or much smaller) than it wound up being for a program or service? Was your behavior inappropriate or unexpected? If something happened that was beyond your ultimate control, like a failed vote for a budget increase or a review board not selecting your grant proposal, how did that impact your plan? What will you do going forward? Will you try again or does it not make sense to right now? It takes a lot of courage to be vulnerable enough, especially if you're in a leadership position, to recognize your limits or to confess that events were legitimately beyond your power or control. That kind of courage deserves respect, and we'd like to think you'll earn respect if you're honest and self-aware when talking about your shortcomings and missteps.

On the other hand, you might be walking into a position where there's baggage to handle that would be lumped on *anyone* who's stepping into those shoes. (See figure 3.2.) It's not specifically aimed at you, and it's not a response to anything you've done wrong (or done right), but you still have to deal with it. What do you do? For one thing, try not to make any assumptions about what people think about you or might be saying behind your back. Don't over-react to negative comments or assume that everyone shares one person's less-than-nice opinions of the folks who've had your job in the past. Give people a chance to express their grievances about how your predecessors did their work or acted toward their colleagues; make them feel heard and see that you care, not that you're taking what they're saying personally or that you're just going to defend the choices of your forebears. Take the time to respond to their concerns meaningfully and with actionable changes you can make: for instance, if members of a department specifically tell you they felt neglected by the person who came before you, make it a point to visit them regularly and give them different options for sharing their ideas and feedback. Their trust may have waned to the point where they don't feel comfortable speaking out in a meeting for fear of repercussions or public shaming, but they might be okay with sharing their thoughts if they're sitting in your office with just you and the door is closed. People respond strongly to past negative experiences at work, just as they do with any other interpersonal relationships in their lives.

FIGURE 3.2
Libraries are old institutions. They've all got their own baggage, both physical and emotional.

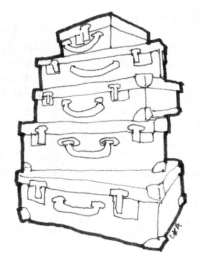

It might take them a while to reset the expectations they formulated with the past person; they've been conditioned, and they won't know until you show them that you'll act differently.

How do you know when trust has been restored? Well, we're sorry to say you probably won't ever really know, or at least you won't ever be done with putting in effort to maintain that trust. You can't do a handful of things once and expect that to satisfy everyone forever. Not only is "everyone" likely to look very different in the course of a few years of departures and arrivals, you're also going to need to show that you aren't just doing lip service. As Brown advises us, small acts build trust, and those small acts over time continue to feed and sustain it. It's up to you to figure out how to make gestures that feel genuine and appropriate to yourself and your colleagues. Whether it's acknowledging whenever things are going right, passing positive feedback along to everyone, making a spreadsheet of everyone's birthdays, or just remembering to ask about a coworker's kids or cats, you don't have to reinvent the wheel here. If you're trying to build trust among colleagues and you're a manager or you can make a suggestion to one—which should cover just about everyone reading this book—you can schedule time for people to do nothing except get to know one another.

Callan is in a department where employees have a weekly thirty-minute block starting at 9:30 on Friday mornings called Friday Fellowship. They drink coffee, bring in a snack to share, and talk about whatever is on their minds, whether it's the weather, something in the news, or a need for recommendations about housing or travel. Especially when new folks join the team, this is a great way to break down the walls of formality and productivity and just be regular ol' people for a bit. The tradition continued on Zoom during COVID-19, and even without the communal cheese Danish, everyone felt a little closer together. The bottom line is you can and should be kind, thoughtful, and truly interested in people's lives. After all, many of them are spending a third of their lives with you.

Now, on to everyone's favorite part of this discussion: What do you do with the folks you can't seem to make any progress with? We mean the people who still glower whenever you approach, whom you overhear talking about you behind your back, or who don't do anything you ask them to do. You know the ones—unless you live in some kind of bizarre, bucolic bubble that we'd love to join you in. We say, "Kill it with kindness" and stick to that plan even if they won't budge an inch. In most library settings, their future with you, or without you, will depend largely on their own choices. You might have the ability to place folks on performance improvement plans, to discipline them based on poor performance, or to document enough of their shortcomings that you might have solid grounds for taking more serious action, but in all likelihood, they will leave on their own volition, if they leave at all. So, with that tricky reality in mind, you will be left with control over only yourself and how you're affected by a problematic person's actions or behavior.

Take it from us: we've been in situations with toxic colleagues and have wanted to bolt or at least wanted answers for why certain attitudes were allowed to exist. We've been in situations with toxic leaders and haven't been sure of what options were available to us for communicating that without risking our jobs (sadly, with this scenario, it's usually best to try to leave if you can). It's not necessarily fair or logical, but sometimes there really isn't anything that can be done to mitigate the source of the toxicity. You can, however, decide how much mental energy and anguish you're willing to spend on someone. You can contextualize the bad actor and think about the other parts of your ecosystem at work that bring you satisfaction. You can consider other job options if that person's behavior truly outweighs what you like about your role. You can explain the situation to people who might have a little more power over the person in question and are willing to go to bat for you behind the scenes. It's not always going to be sunshine and roses, and it's not with flippant naïveté that we suggest you leave your job for a different one, as if that's ever a simple process. We just don't want you to be captive to someone else's bad behavior or to burn out from your frustrations.

About gossip: Have you ever been a part of a clique that has little else to talk about other than the latest drama with so-and-so? Yeah, we have too. That can be fun or cathartic in the moment, but in the long run, be careful about how much time you spend fixating on someone who probably has little to do with the best and brightest parts of your job. We understand these sessions can be super-satisfying, but they don't often lead to any change. Try to keep your bigger picture goals in mind. Negativity breeds more negativity, and you can be the place where it stops.

HIRING

Librarianship is not a diverse field, and we need to stop the lip service and start taking that extremely seriously. As of 2012, upward of 80 percent of credentialed librarians in the United States classified themselves as white. In a 2016 article published in the journal *In the Library with the Lead Pipe*," Jennifer Vinopal compares a figure of 88 percent white librarians in the United States with a 63.7 percent white census estimate of the total population.[2] Black librarians make up 5.2 percent of the field in a country with a 12.6 percent black population; other racial and ethnic groups find even lower proportional representation. And this homogeneity doesn't stop there: another article in *In the Library with the Lead Pipe*, A.S. Galvan's "Soliciting Performance, Hiding Bias: Whiteness in Librarianship," offers a useful definition of *whiteness* as encompassing, not just what we mean when we say racially white, but also all that is "heterosexual, capitalist, and middle class."[3] The authors of this book are both white, middle-class, cisgender women; the statistics lead us to suspect many of you holding it are as well.

Recruiting Inclusively

For those of us in management, a step on the organizational ladder that is held predominantly by white women, we have much work to do. We need to actively recruit job candidates from underrepresented groups. It's not enough to put postings on the usual websites and electronic discussion lists and ask our colleagues to pass along the word to folks in their networks. "Send staff to attend conferences or meetings that individuals from underrepresented groups attend and encourage them to think of your organization as a place that would welcome their applications," Vinopal suggests in her article, and "recruit staff who are already credentialed but who, for whatever reason, haven't made their way into professional positions."[4] The same goes for encouraging library support staff to consider getting their credentials and then meaningfully follow through on providing mentorship and support.

Also writing for *In the Library with the Lead Pipe*, April Hathcock provides library leaders with action items to "fight whiteness in our diversity initiatives."[5] She recommends volunteering to organize and execute diversity efforts, including questioning and reworking barriers to entry for employment, scholarship, or career development programs. Hathcock also advocates for formal mentoring and navigational assistance for new library workers, to help them understand and acknowledge professional whiteness, as well as informal mentoring through social media. We need to create systems of support and collaboration at every level, from our own workplaces to our professional organizations. It's also essential for us to contend with the library as a structure built within a context of historical oppression. "The fantasy of the library still holds some sway as a place that is somehow not only removed from white supremacy but is even antithetical to it in some way," Michelle Santamaria writes in a 2020 *Library Trends* article.[6] "[It's] framed by many as one of the last bastions of democracy, which is in turn also conceptualized as free of white supremacy."

Managers must build these priorities and goals into strategic plans and expectations for all employees. "Libraries have to open their arms to all perspectives and experiences," the ACRL wrote in its 2012 report on diversity and cultural competency standards.[7] "That requires competency in matters of cultural pluralism that are not intuitive and must be learned, like any other essential skill." *Cultural competency*, as defined by the report, is "a congruent set of behaviors, attitudes, and policies that enable a person or group to work effectively in cross-cultural situations." To achieve cultural competency, staff need to examine how their social identities and cultural heritage influence their own assumptions and values, and how these identities and assumptions in turn influence their interactions with colleagues and patrons. In the absence of these efforts, we're likely to see a continuing trend of low morale among nonwhite librarians. Kaetrena Davis Kendrick and Ione T. Damasco's 2020 paper on the subject in *Library Trends* demonstrates we've got a long way to go: "The profession continues to struggle with consistently framing, promoting, and supporting the library profession and library spaces as welcoming to and safe for marginalized racial, cultural, and ethnic groups."[8]

Library leaders can encourage this self-awareness by generating conversations about discrimination, bias, and stereotyping. They can bring speakers and workshop leaders to staff development days and other library programming that prompts this dialogue; they can pay for and provide access to continuing education materials and books; they can share stories and prompt discussions that "acknowledge how fears, ignorance, and the '-isms' have influenced [our] attitudes, beliefs, and behaviors."[9] We're not sure of its origin, but the phrase "Take space, make space" is a good framing to start with as your library works to encourage dialogue and challenge whiteness. The idea here is to ask people to be mindful of privileged identities they may hold—taking the time to understand how and when these privileges can grant them a louder voice—and to intentionally create an environment where others who might not share those identities can feel comfortable contributing to the conversation.

Searching for Specific Skills

You might be wondering about the specific skills or knowledge areas to look out for when you're hiring. It's difficult to answer this question without knowing more about the position and the library you're hiring for, so rather than give you a prescribed list of skills, we offer here some broader qualities to incorporate when you're writing job descriptions and to inquire about when interviewing prospective staff:

- previous work or volunteer experience with underserved populations, community organizations, or other groups for which understanding and responding to underrepresented perspectives is essential
- specific interest in and/or previous experience with inclusion efforts, such as generating programming and book displays, focusing on collection development, or partnering with other community groups to identify opportunities for outreach
- knowledge of your current strategic plan (if you have one) and the community you serve, whether that's a municipality, college campus, or business
- strong opinions

About that last one: There are many aspects of the inclusivity, usability, accessibility, and clunkiness of libraries that people should be able to weigh in on and criticize constructively, provided you give them a safe space to air their thoughts without repercussions. A favorite interview question of ours is, "If you could change one thing about the way libraries provide service to patrons, what would it be?"

We hope it goes without saying that you shouldn't tick off skills from a checklist and toss a résumé into a yes or no pile just based on that. Specific skills aren't going to be what helps you and your team endure change, but instead the willingness to dismantle things, to be curious and self-aware—those are the traits that have lasting value.

On the flip side, if you're writing a cover letter for a new job, be yourself and speak to your passion. What brings you to work every day is what we want to hear about as hiring managers. We want to know that when the going gets tough, you'll be able to zoom out to the end goal, whether that's helping to reopen a renovated branch or assisting patrons with opening e-books on their phones. Think about what you'd say if you were asked to describe what you want to be doing in five or ten years. Hiring managers are aware that they won't retain most of their employees for more than a few years, but they want to bring on board people who have a clear vision for the short term and can self-start right away.

For those of us in managerial positions, we should ask ourselves what we can do to rework our criteria for successful candidates and acknowledge that our assessment of prospective employees—just like sharing job postings on the same mailing lists and passing the word along in our networks—is influenced by propagation of the status quo. When interviewers talk about a candidate's *cultural fit*, what do they mean? Is the idea that librarianship is a calling an excuse to pay low wages? Do we acknowledge that participating in professional development and attending conferences requires financial privilege? How are we helping with that? Are we coming into the recruitment process with the notion that diversity is a problem we need to solve? Are we acknowledging librarianship is not somehow exempt from white supremacy? Those of us in positions of power need to grapple with these questions and hold ourselves accountable for the change we claim we want to see in the field.

DEDICATED EFFORTS TOWARD INCLUSION

In recent years, many libraries have begun to approach adding new services through an *equity lens*. Countless definitions can be found on the web, but we think the version from Multnomah County, Oregon, is among the best: an equity lens is a "transformative quality improvement tool used to improve planning, decision-making, and resource allocation leading to more racially equitable policies and programs."[10] Though the metaphor of a lens can be problematic—suggesting something you can apply or take on and off, as opposed to something you should use all the time—the idea for libraries is that staff members should take time to think carefully about inclusion, approachability, and audience when they're planning programs, adding to the collection, and performing all other services.

Another way of looking at it is through a framework called design justice. Created by the Design Justice Network, a collective of designers and community organizers, design justice seeks to "rethink design processes that too often reproduce race, class, and gender inequality, and question the ways that design practices undergird or destabilize systems of structural and historic oppression."[11] Though library workers don't often think of themselves as designers, we do design services, collections, programs, and more. The Design Justice Network has created a list of ten principles to help guide this critical rethinking process, including "We work towards sustainable, community-led and -controlled outcomes." [12] This centering of the library's users is crucial in assessing what needs are going unmet and using what is already working in the community to guide new efforts.

The Houston Public Library has made dedicated efforts to ensure their services reach the underserved. Their bookmobile is actually a "computer classroom on wheels." As described on the library's website, the HPL Mobile Express is

> a new concept in the delivery of library services, bringing access to technology and a number of programs to high-need neighborhoods. Services provided include literacy programs, workforce development training, computer training, access to technology, homework help, enrichment programs, English as Second Language classes, after school programs, and library card registration.[13]

The vehicle is equipped with "12 desktop computers, 10 laptops, wi-fi and a large-screen smart board for instruction, various programs, and more."

Notice that this effort to increase equity is a bookmobile, meaning it requires engaging people outside of the library. We should consider what that implies about how welcoming or known (or not) our spaces are. We should also think about how to meet people where they are rather than expecting them to come to us. A few libraries are doing projects with local laundromats that go beyond just making books available by sponsoring storytimes and other events for kids. In the Boston area, libraries are starting to work with medical centers and large hospitals to provide similar outreach in common areas, inside and outside, weather permitting. Assisted living and Section 8 housing centers are eager for librarians to do more outreach, whether it's in the form of showing people how to access electronic resources or teaching computer skills. If the coordinators or volunteers at these places haven't asked your staff to come by yet, it's likely because they are even more pressed for time and resources than your library is. But they are vital allies in serving the underserved.

To ensure there is specific energy, time, and resources committed to service to the underserved and to EDI (equity, diversity, and inclusion) initiatives, library leadership needs to solidify these goals in a strategic plan, discuss how to delegate specific tasks, and hire for new positions or look for skill sets that will help with these efforts. Without administrative support, these efforts quickly fizzle out or do not lead to any lasting structural change. Another likely avenue for offering outreach services is to investigate partnerships with other community efforts centered on racial equity and social justice. For example, the Madison Public Library in Wisconsin has joined the city's

> deliberate, focused and organized effort called the Racial Equity and Social Justice Initiative (RESJI). One of the guiding principles . . . is authentic, ongoing public engagement and participation, with the goal of changing the culture of our city—including addressing institutional racism.[14]

On its website, the library provides toolkits and suggested reading materials created with the library's community partners to further work and learning in Madison and beyond. Another example is the Government Alliance on Race and Equity (GARE), a national effort to "achieve equity and advance opportunities for all."[15] GARE has chapters throughout the United States; one might exist in the community you serve. If you're a manager, introduce yourself to the people working on these efforts (or delegate this to another person on your staff) and ask how your library can help.

NOTES

1. Brené Brown, "The Anatomy of Trust," *SuperSoul Sessions*, season 1, episode 102, Oprah.com video, originally aired October 9, 2015, www.oprah.com/own-super-soul-sunday/Brene-Brown-The-Anatomy-of-Trust-Video.
2. Jennifer Vinopal, "The Quest for Diversity in Library Staffing: From Awareness to Action," *In the Library with the Lead Pipe*, January 13, 2016, www.inthelibrarywiththeleadpipe.org/2016/quest-for-diversity/.
3. A.S. Galvan, "Soliciting Performance, Hiding Bias: Whiteness and Librarianship," *In the Library with the Lead Pipe*, June 3, 2015, www.inthelibrarywiththeleadpipe.org/2015/soliciting-performance-hiding-bias-whiteness-and-librarianship.
4. Vinopal, "Quest for Diversity."
5. April Hathcock, "White Librarianship in Blackface: Diversity Initiatives in LIS," *In the Library with the Lead Pipe*, October 7, 2015, www.inthelibrarywiththeleadpipe.org/2015/lis-diversity/.
6. Michele R. Santamaria, "Concealing White Supremacy through Fantasies of the Library: Economies of Affect at Work," *Library Trends* 68, no. 3 (2020): 435, https://muse.jhu.edu/article/752706.
7. Association of College and Research Libraries (ACRL), "Diversity Standards: Cultural Competency for Academic Libraries (2012)," American Library Association, May 4, 2012, www.ala.org/acrl/standards/diversity.

8. Kaetrena Davis Kendrick and Ione T. Damasco, "Low Morale in Ethnic and Racial Minority Academic Librarians: An Experiential Study," *Library Trends* 68, no. 2 (2019): 208. https://muse.jhu.edu/article/746745.

9. ACRL, "Diversity Standards."

10. Multnomah County, Office of Diversity and Equity, "Equity and Empowerment Lens," https://multco.us/diversity-equity/equity-and-empowerment-lens.

11. Design Justice Network, "If We Want Design to Be a Tool for Liberation, We'll Need More Than Good Intentions," Op-Ed, *AIGA Eye On Design*, July 22, 2020, https://eyeondesign.aiga.org/for-design-to-truly-be-a-tool-for-liberation-were -going-to-need-more-than-just-good-intentions/.

12. Design Justice Network, "Design Justice Network Principles," last updated Summer 2018, https://designjustice.org/read-the-principles.

13. Houston Public Library, "Community Engagement," https://houstonlibrary.org/ our-partners/community-engagement.

14. Madison Public Library, "Racial Equity Resources," www.madisonpubliclibrary .org/racial-equity/resources.

15. Government Alliance on Race and Equity, "Who We Are," www.racialequity alliance.org/about/who-we-are/.

4
Library Technology

Why is technology in libraries so important? We'd like to think this goes without saying today, and there is plenty of data out there to underscore how much the public relies on libraries to provide access to and training on technology. Callan used to work in a public library system with three branches serving a population of about 59,000. In 2019 the reference staff fielded around 2,650 questions about technology per year, saw up to 8,000 desktop computer uses per month, and averaged more than 4,000 Wi-Fi sessions per month. According to data collected by the Massachusetts Board of Library Commissioners, the statewide number of sessions on library-owned computers *alone* was around 5.25 million in 2018.[1] During the COVID-19 crisis, the closure of libraries led to patrons flocking to library parking lots to jump on the Wi-Fi,[2] and some libraries went so far as to add additional Wi-Fi *to* those parking lots.[3]

In 2019 Pew Research Center released survey results that showed a majority of Americans could not answer questions about tech companies or online security and privacy,[4] showcasing another set of digital literacy skills that libraries should work on building among members of their communities. Given the critical and ubiquitous role the tech giants of today play in our lives, from shopping to both personal and professional communication to entertainment and news and so much more, we owe it to our patrons to help them better understand the evolving information landscape of the twenty-first century. Not only do many of these companies shy away from providing customer support or training—have *you* ever tried to call Facebook?—but, save for verbose and confusing user agreements, they also aren't exactly forthcoming about their collection and redistribution of user data, which is in many ways an affront to the patron privacy we librarians are sworn to protect.

Beyond libraries, there aren't many other venues in society for educating the public on the trade-offs they're making in order to use the websites, services, and apps that dominate the web today. While we are not suggesting that libraries should dissuade all patrons from using the many mainstream web platforms that rely on personal and behavioral data to turn a profit (e.g., social media sites, e-mail providers, online retailers, and more), we do think education, discussion, and criticism about these issues should be encouraged. Whether focusing on basic cybersecurity skills to help patrons avoid identity theft or inviting authors who study how the surveillance of private citizens fuels the internet economy, we need to improve our patrons' understanding of these technologies and the companies who created them, especially now that they have become so embedded in our lives.

Zeroing in more specifically to the technologies we rely on, both to do our own jobs and to help patrons do whatever they've come to us to do, this chapter focuses on the combination of physical hardware and related software systems that are unique to a library setting. Although other fields and organizations use similar tech in certain applications, we have a mix that's all our own, including retail-like inventory control peripherals on our workstations as well as a range of devices for the public to use or borrow. We also describe some alternatives to common workflows, suggesting tools and techniques aimed at improved communication, data collection, and other means of keeping your wits about you as things continue to change.

UX AND LIBRARY TECHNOLOGY

This section is going to sound like complaining. To be blunt, the experience of using most library technologies is bad—but it's important to unpack why. User experience and one of its key components, usability, are often improved more by identifying what's wrong than by identifying what's right. By acknowledging and understanding the pain points and limitations of what we've got today, we can work toward improvements on scales both large and small.

Think about the software and hardware most library staff use to complete the fundamental tasks of their jobs, and think about the conversations surrounding them. Take integrated library systems (ILSs) and catalogs. How many times have you heard a particular ILS described, with or without a reluctant sigh, as "the lesser of two evils," "the devil you know," or "not the best but it gets the job done"? How about library print vending systems (i.e., systems whereby patrons release print jobs sent to a queue by paying some amount of money)? Do you have one that you love, or do you have one that makes your blood boil and seems broken all the time but you tolerate it because, as much as you hate every second of dealing with it, you still have to offer this basic service to your patrons?

There aren't many competitors working in the library vendor space for a few reasons. The biggest one will not shock you, and it's that despite the number of libraries in the world, there's not a lot of money to be made in the library software business. Most libraries can't pay up for flashy tech, and the tech itself doesn't get developed to be flashy anyway. At the time of this writing, library tech is still being built on data models and structures that were created more than fifty years ago. Most commercial ILSs, no matter what minimal modern skin or font you slap on them, have creaky bones underneath; the records inside of them are still digital versions of the paper cards they replaced.

Libraries also suffer from being a bit of a misfit with their service model. Developments that have vastly improved the usability and customizability of commercial point-of-sale systems and self-checkout terminals don't work the same way in our environment, where the items taken out always have to be brought back. Imagine the number of stores that now use the Square checkout app on a tablet with their special card readers connected; they all have similar needs, so they can use the same solution. Also, unlike retail stores that are all part of the same chain, even libraries that are in neighboring towns in the same network or consortium may have completely different self-checkout machines or means of inventory control (specifically, RFID [radio frequency identification] vs. non-RFID locations).

Many library procedures that we consider to be normal workflows are just plain user-unfriendly for nonlibrarians who aren't expecting friction when they're using technology. The complexity and the inconvenience of quite a few library apps and services are easily enough to turn patrons away. Take accessing e-books, for example. Librarians know the world of publishing is fraught with arguments over embargoes, limited-access licenses, and price-jacking by companies who know they have us in a vice. But how many patrons think about that when they see the sixteen-week estimated turnaround time for an electronic copy of a new bestseller? How many faculty members think, "Oh, I should be sure to ask the library for unlimited simultaneous uses for that e-book I need to assign for next week's reading"? The situation defies common sense. It's no wonder why patrons turn to paid services to access e-books or to less-than-legal ways of obtaining content that lives behind a paywall.

So what's a librarian to do? These problems might seem insurmountable, and in the short term, some of them might well be. But there are solutions for others. We can simplify our offerings, taking the pressure off of staff to do constant triage and to focus instead on providing specialized or individual help where it's needed. We can stand stronger together and leverage partnerships, like networks and consortia, to have more say in the design of the systems being sold to us. Perhaps most important of all, we can start piece by piece, and we can start tomorrow.

We can't fix all of our hardware and software problems overnight, but we can start thinking about our technologies as a system of components that impact the experience of using our libraries. The best place to start is at ground zero: the act of circulation. What is it like for patrons to check out books? On the flip side, what is it like for staff to check them back in?

Let's talk about search behavior. Like it or not, library catalogs and electronic resources suffer from digital clunkiness and lack of usability. It can be difficult for patrons to know what you have access to and how to find things in many different types of library products, ranging from discovery services and article aggregators to catalogs of physical and online materials. In chapter 5, we delve deeper into findability in the physical building, but here's a good place to start training yourself to think about it as we chop this decades-long dilemma into more manageable parts.

It's scary and intimidating to think, "Our systems are so outdated and unusable that it's no wonder patrons get fed up." How many people would be affected and how much money would have to go into fixing all of that? How many years would it take? Slow down for a second. You might not have control over your catalog's user interface, but you likely have control over your own website. We bet you can make the beginning steps a little easier and less confusing. You can drop the jargon in your explanations and navigation menus, and you can run them past laypersons for feedback. And you may not know it, but you've got an ace up your sleeve: *you can make it simpler for patrons to get help finding things.* One of the many resources libraries have that Google, Facebook, and Amazon do not is a friendly expert on the other end of a phone call, e-mail, or chat message.

Remember, too, that some of the limitations of library systems are intentional, and some of these limitations might be at odds with what users expect. Callan currently works at a college where the library circulates camera equipment, some of which goes missing on occasion mostly due to benevolent absentmindedness. Students wish there was a way to know who checked out a camera most recently so they could get in touch with the current or last borrower, but library catalogs are built to protect patrons' privacy so that information isn't made publicly available. Similarly, most ILS vendors collect patrons' reading histories only if they actively and intentionally opt in, a choice that more and more patrons want in this age of past order histories and personalized recommendations. This is a teachable moment: Do your patrons know that you're protecting their privacy by operating this way? Do they know why you, as a librarian, think that's important, even though it comes at the cost of some convenience?

This brings us to a related problem, which is that librarians often think the rules that apply to other kinds of organizations and businesses—those which make a profit, for instance—don't make sense for us to follow. That is true and important in some ways, as in the case of privacy versus convenience that we just mentioned. However, though we need to be careful, we can still learn from companies that may not share our ethical standards or service models. We shouldn't go reinventing the wheels of user experience trends established by businesses that boast whole UX departments to build their interfaces and products, and we shouldn't ignore the research being done by those businesses on customer service trends in the twenty-first century. Underlying motives aside, they have more money, more researchers, and more time to throw at this topic than we do. Libraries aren't on the cutting edge of technology, but many businesses try their best to be.

Take Microsoft's "2018 State of Global Customer Service Report," available for download after you (ironically!) fork over your contact and employer information.[5] In this document, Microsoft Research presents key findings from a survey of 5,000 people in the United States, Japan, Brazil, Germany, and the United Kingdom aimed at identifying how brands can differentiate themselves from the competition. Substitute *libraries* for *brands* and consider how the research shows that loyalty to brands is closely tied to customer service quality. How might libraries build their brands? Through logos, individualized library cards, and consistent signage and graphic design. Also, 70 percent of respondents said they have a more favorable view of companies that "offer or contact [them] with proactive customer service notifications."[6] How might we engage in these proactive notifications? Newsletters or receipts printed or e-mailed with a footer about upcoming events might work. You don't need to get fancy; even basic things like hold pickup or due date notices are push notifications.

Another finding of note in Microsoft's survey is that only 39 percent of respondents thought that getting answers by engaging with customer service is becoming easier. Those surveyed indicated that the most important aspect of a good customer service experience is "getting my issue resolved in a single interaction (no matter the length of time)" and the most frustrating aspect is getting a "representative [who] lacks the ability or knowledge to resolve my issue."[7] What might we take away from this?

Again, let's start by breaking down the complexity of what's being reported into more solvable pieces. There are two main pieces here: (1) access to help and (2) knowledgeability of the helper. How can we make it easier to access help? As we mentioned earlier in the chapter, libraries can offer chat or text services, responding to overall trends in how people engage with companies today. Indeed, Microsoft's study found that 21 percent of respondents between the ages of eighteen and thirty-four said live chat was their preferred channel for customer service.[8]

Libraries can also use online ticketing systems or solutions other than just plain e-mail for better tracking of questions and answers. They can simplify their phone menu options or make it easier to get through to a human when patrons are not able to navigate the choices or the choices don't address what they're calling about. Microsoft's study found that phone calls were still the preferred channel for customer service across all age groups, so don't discount how important this medium can be in an age that seems dominated by e-mail and text.

Moving on to the knowledgeability of the helper, to use the language of the survey questions, getting issues resolved in a single interaction most likely depends on whether the representative has the ability or knowledge to resolve an issue. How can we ensure our frontline staff have the power and understanding to be able to resolve the majority of customer service issues? Start by figuring out what the most common customer service issues are. Cross-train staff so they know how to answer most questions that come their way or, at least, can say exactly who can answer the question if they don't know themselves. Write clear, simple policies that don't require years of experience to be able to understand and follow. Make those policies easily findable so staff can refer to them when ambiguous situations arise. If you have weird or specific rules, like only one certain person can override fines or refill the paper in the public printer, ask yourself if it makes sense to keep these bottlenecks in place or if they have a negative impact on service. Encourage and empower your staff to do their best not to let a patron come away from a customer service encounter disappointed or leave the library having had a bad experience—possibly never to return.

STRONGER TOGETHER

It's a tale as old as time, or at least as old as the widespread adoption of automated library systems and online catalogs: external IT departments don't always love or even understand the library—we go deeper into this later in the chapter. Libraries were often online before other campus or municipal departments were, a situation leading to silos that have persisted for decades. The time has come to try to break down the silos. You can benefit from specialized expertise, cooperative purchasing, and stabilizing your infrastructure by working more closely with your local IT group. This means cheaper and faster computers and internet service, which means happier staff and patrons.

You might also want to consider joining an automated network of other libraries in your area if you aren't in one yet, and if you are in one, you might want to think about how to get more out of that partnership. This landscape varies pretty widely from state to state, but where we work in Massachusetts, we have several networks of varying sizes that include both public and academic libraries. The big benefits of our networks are simplified cooperative borrowing, shared catalogs, technical support and subsidized telecommunications equipment (in some cases), and group purchasing abilities. Being a network member typically gives your patrons easier access to far more items than you could ever provide to them on your own; it also can fill gaps in your staffing and make it less daunting to negotiate deals with vendors.

We can't help but mention the importance of the other part of networking: the kind you do with your colleagues in local interest groups and communities of practice, during visits to neighboring libraries, and at conferences both near and far. You can get help for just about any kind of problem you're running into from other technology librarians (or people who've assumed that role on their staffs), and most people who are working in our field are doing so because they want to share information, not hide their solutions and ideas. There's no sense reinventing wheels when there are existing wheels you could stand to learn from nearby.

If you're considering using a new vendor or service, ask to be put in touch with local fellow clients and be sure to reach out to them. Try to get an honest take on the pros and cons. Find out if any missteps were made on either side of the transaction that you might be able to avoid. If you're reading this and feeling like there's nobody out there who can help you, consult fellow library workers on social media or post to any of the numerous library mailing lists; you can also reach out by starting your own groups or mailing lists. Don't be afraid to ask for help when you need it.

Consider speaking at conferences, at the regional level to start with, maybe by doing a short session (twenty minutes or less) or cofacilitating a breakout session. If you're speaking, you can guide the conversation and find others who are dealing with or are interested in the same issues. This can lead to opportunities to participate on a larger scale by joining sections within the host organization or by serving on the conference committee to help shape programming in a way that reflects your interests.

The 80/20 Rule

The 80/20 rule, also called the Pareto principle, states that for many events, 80 percent of the effects come from 20 percent of the causes.* For instance, some business leaders claim that 80 percent of their sales come from 20 percent of their customers. We're taking this in a slightly different direction by suggesting that it's okay to aim for solutions that will satisfy 80 percent of patrons' needs and to deal with the other 20 percent on a case-by-case basis.

Imagine the computers available for patron use at a public library. Most patrons use these machines to browse the web, print out bus tickets or tax forms, or fill out job applications. Every now and then, you might get someone who wants to do serious photo editing or stream ultra-high-definition videos or kids who are begging you to install the latest battle royale game. If you apply the 80/20 rule and focus first on the needs of the many, you can meet the majority of patron needs with very low-power, low-cost options that might be light on processing power but are perfectly capable of releasing print jobs or browsing the web. We give a more specific suggestion on how this can play out in a later section on public computers and printers.

We've often heard that libraries are expected to be all things to all people, but that's not a realistic plan for a manageable future. Especially with regard to technology, libraries cannot be expected to fulfill 100 percent of patrons' needs and to supply 100 percent of all emerging technologies just as they cannot be expected to keep a copy of every book ever published on their shelves. By identifying the essentials unique to each community and treating exceptions as the rarities they are, libraries can keep their core offerings simple but responsive to the majority of their users.

* Jim Chappelow, "Pareto Principle," Investopedia.com, August 29, 2019, www.investopedia.com/terms/p/paretoprinciple.asp.

SOFTWARE

Integrated Library System

At the bottom of everything, you need an ILS you can count on. It might seem silly to point out something so fundamental, but in some libraries (and we have worked in them!), this component that is so crucial to operations is unreliable. Especially now, in the 2020s, given the new startup options that have cropped up in the market over the past five years or so, a temperamental ILS is a risk that shouldn't be dismissed. Though it's tempting to investigate the possibilities of a well-marketed, unconventional competitor over the big names in the business, do your homework about what you're being sold, who's building it, and what kind of support there is.

As with purchasing any other form of new technology, you may run the risk of being the guinea pigs for a system that's not yet ready for prime time, and you might be bankrolling the development of a product that will be sold to other libraries. If you think this might be going on, don't hesitate to ask the vendor. You might be able to use it to your advantage (such as with early adopter discounts).

Keep in mind that changing to a different system, whether it's from an old company or a new startup, is going to impact staff experience, speed, and familiarity; the experience patrons have of using the library will be impacted as well while the staff learn to use the software. Changing your user and inventory management system is going to reverberate throughout the organization, so if you choose to do this, make sure the benefits outweigh the disruptions. Think it through carefully: What will your patrons and staff gain? What will they lose? Forcing changes that don't have clear benefits and don't meaningfully add to goals, with all the extra work and learning curves, is going to feel like an unnecessary attack on your colleagues.

It might be tempting to try your hand at being a pioneer, but you don't need to be banging your head against the wall trying to troubleshoot and accomplish basic tasks in the name of innovation. This will only frustrate staff, and they'll pass along those frustrations to your patrons, who will in turn get frustrated as well.

Catalog Interfaces and Discovery Layers

Many catalog interfaces haven't changed much since they found their way to the web, though a few companies are trying to reinvent the idea of a library catalog. One such company is BiblioCommons (www.bibliocommons.com), which boasts the ability to search and display content beyond a library's holdings, indexing things like events and classes as well. Options for customization and recommended content are another feature of newfangled catalogs, which brings up questions of data retention and privacy.

Discovery layers, multiplatform search engines that are generally used to comb through many electronic resources at once, have become increasingly common in recent years, but they often carry a high price tag and leave a lot to be desired. While the appeal of having a Google-like service in libraries is certainly understandable, the search results turned up by discovery layers aren't the easiest to read, and for many users, the heavily text-based nature of such interfaces isn't particularly attractive.

The bottom line here is that our technology for finding library materials has a long way to go before it offers a good user experience for nonlibrarians. In the longer term, we should push vendors for user-friendly mobile solutions that anyone can search from anywhere, with interfaces that are inviting and reflective of broader aesthetic trends in apps and on the web. For now, though, libraries can leverage the range of available web publishing tools to pinch-hit for their catalogs and other resources or offerings that might be hard to surface. Discovery layers are great assets in theory, but what they promise is findability, which can be addressed through other means like good marketing and improved web design. We talk more about this in an upcoming section about library websites.

HARDWARE

Let's take a step back from the ILS and catalog and look at all that stuff you've got plugged in on your circulation desk, starting with computers. How old are they? What's the plan (if there is one) for how and when they get replaced? Who does those replacements (library, town, or campus IT)? If you don't know the answers to these questions, it's time to start asking around.

"Wait," you might be saying, "what does this have to do with library UX?" Great question! If your circulation desk computers have been around for more than a few years, they're probably going to be knocking at death's door soon, if they're not already. We've seen computers in some libraries that struggle to find the power to open a web browser in addition to the library's ILS. That type of situation will prevent staff from doing much in the way of multitasking, which is something busy front desk workers should always be doing: switching between handling e-mail, searching the web, and using various modules in the ILS. Old computers are bad enough for the staff-side experience, but how do you think a computer crash or a painstakingly slow answer looks and feels on the other side of the desk? Having the first people patrons encounter in the library feeling ready to take a hammer to their workstations is not a good look for any of the services you provide.

Replace Your Replacement Plan

We are fully aware of the financial limitations confronted by many institutions and municipalities. Still, we offer here some rules of thumb and basic ideas in hopes of helping you stay out in front of planned obsolescence and prevent your circulation staff from tossing a monitor out a window. Though it's very specific to staff technology and workflows, we wrote this list with user experience in mind.

1. Get on a replacement cycle that plans for every computer you buy or lease to be phased out according to a clearly defined schedule. At the time of this writing, four years per computer is a fairly common estimate that should keep you ahead of obsolescence.

2. Stagger the replacements of computers; for example, if you're in a system with sixty staff machines, your staff or IT group would replace only fifteen or twenty of those at a time. Don't just wing this; give every department and staff member a heads-up about the replacement well in advance, and ask them to weigh in on the best times to make the change without disrupting their workflow.

3. If this hasn't been done yet and you have the opportunity for change, normalize staff computers with those used by the rest of the departments in your town or on your campus. Large-scale purchasing helps keep costs down. Standardizing what you've got with what all the other departments have will make it easier for you to get help from external IT groups—if you have that luxury!

4. *Don't forget everything else that's plugged into these computers.* More detail in the next section.

Your ability to offer good service relies on the ability of staff to be able to perform the basic tasks required to provide that service. With the exception of very small libraries or those that haven't been automated yet, computers are at the core of how we do our work. Making sure your staff are using healthy, up-to-date machines that are quick and easy to support will mean you have fewer issues that disrupt service as it's happening, and fewer issues that front-line staff can't learn how to fix on their own. We might not all be thrilled about it, but we are all tech librarians now.

Bar Code Scanners, RFID Pads, Receipt Printers, and Whatever Else

Have you ever gone into a convenience store with an old-school point-of-sale system—not one of those slick "Square readers plugged into an iPad" joints, but a register with a cash drawer, a bar code scanner, and a receipt printer? At the time of this writing, the best example we can think of is on display at many 7-Elevens around Boston. It's usually a mess of twisted-up cables and dust, maybe with a nice coating of coffee or the Big Gulp du jour. (See figure 4.1.)

Callan once worked at a library with circulation stations that made their counterparts at 7-Eleven look like the handiwork of a master interior designer. Crammed underneath a monolithic wood-and-marble desk that wasn't built to have computers in, on, or anywhere near it were cables running from the PC to a tangle of outdated peripherals on the countertop. There was a receipt printer with a parallel port output, which is no longer something installed on most towers manufactured today. There was a bar code scanner with a PS2 connection (the kind on your antique mouse) that required a chunky USB dongle. The mouse and keyboard were from a different major computer manufacturer that the town hadn't done business with for at least the past five years; they were half-broken and dirt-logged hand-me-downs. And last but not least, the RFID pad (or antenna), revolutionary at the time of its installation, was of the first generation commercially available in the United States. As it was 2017 when this tangled web was discovered, it had been there for nearly a decade. The most damning thing of it all, though, was the number of zip ties lashing these wires together, pulled completely taut, as if to say, "This is fine for the rest of forever, right?" Wrong. So wrong.

Even in a town with deep coffers, these items, all fundamental to the processes of circulation and technical services—the core of what libraries do—hadn't been replaced in a decade or more. We don't want to dwell on why that happened, but we do want to call this out as a warning not to forget about the importance of these deeply unsexy gadgets in the face of the emerging technologies and shiny objects we're forever trying to stay on top of. Just as we recommended for computers, we say create a schedule of replacement for these things too. When in doubt for a time frame, five years seems like a good starting place to at least check in on the health and status of these tools. If

FIGURE 4.1
No matter what you're working on, try to take the long view. Think of every tech manage-ment choice as a chance to plug in your cables neatly: it might take a little longer to do it right, but it'll make your life a whole lot easier when the time comes to replace things.

---

you're considering or in the process of RFID implementation, make sure to keep this replacement cycle in mind when buying or leasing equipment. Many vendors are willing to work with you on this, which has the benefit of helping amortize costs and reduce sticker shock as well as build replacement right into the terms of your business with them.

What does this have to do with user experience? At this point, we're hope-ful you'll recognize the general refrain: tech that's reliable leads to happier staff; happier staff are better suited to help your patrons because they can provide consistent, stable service. As customer service demands increase and usage patterns tend toward community in addition to collections, we have less and less time to waste on cursing out our printers or wondering why our bar code scanners work only half the time.

Public Computers and Printers

For those of you working in public libraries, here's where you'll find a fun combo of "one of the most important parts of your service" and "the hardest part to get right." The difficulties of public computing and printing are largely a result of what's available from vendors in this space, which is not great, to say the least. Many times management programs available for library comput-ers haven't changed much in a long while; they are clunky and aesthetically behind the curve, plus they generally require extra software to protect patron privacy and keep computers usable.

In the 80/20 Rule box earlier in the chapter, we suggested trying to find a simplified solution that will work for 80 percent of your regular users, then handling exceptions as best as you can when they come up. Let's look at some specific examples. Thin clients, which are simple computers that don't have a ton of power but are designed to be easy to maintain, can save you a ton of time and money spent on additional software for keeping machines clean. We also know of libraries that use distributions of Linux on public computers and laptops, prompting patrons to use a guest mode that wipes sessions into oblivion upon log-out.

To accommodate the needs of the 20 percent, some libraries offer one or a handful of multimedia stations, either laptops or desktops, with increased memory or processing power and loaded with photo-, audio-, and video-editing software. This way, you don't have to break the bank with licenses or equipment or overburden staff with the Sisyphean task of trying to keep a whole fleet of high-end computers in the exact same condition they were in the day they were installed.

Printers in libraries are—well, where do we begin? Printers everywhere aren't great. In an episode of the technology podcast *Reply All*, the show's hosts speak to Joshua Rothman, an online editor for the *New Yorker*, who describes the "Google Scholar rabbit hole" he went down trying to figure out why printers are so bad in an era of tech advancement and possibility.[9] Rothman explains that part of the problem is that printers are getting smaller and smaller, but they still have to accommodate some pretty impressive internal engineering as paper makes its way through the vacuums, twists, and turns inside. He notes, too, that paper itself has subtle variations from package and package and sheet to sheet. Rothman optimistically offers that printers aren't really getting worse; they're able to print much faster than ever before, but that means they also are more prone to jams because they're expected to do more printing.

This is all to say that printing in the library is especially difficult to manage because of the volume of output. Public libraries are, in most cases, the cheapest shop in town for printing by the page, and patrons know that and love it. The other problem is paying for printing, which many libraries handle through an automatic vending system that is often maintained by an external company. There's no panacea we can offer here, but we have a few suggestions. Let's start with the most pie-in-the-sky one first: we know of at least one library in Massachusetts that has decided to have its Friends of the Library group fund all public printing. There goes your need for a payment system. That is probably not a viable choice for many of us, but it's worth chewing it over.

Barring that, you could switch to a staff release system whereby print jobs are put in a queue to be released by staff. That's not a great option for busy libraries, so if that seems impossible, try to invest in credit card readers if you don't yet have them on terminals—but only if it makes sense. If you don't do enough printing to justify the investment or if your budget is too restrictive, you should nevertheless do what you can to help people use your system. Know where the closest ATMs in town are, and if you have cash on hand in the building from fine collections or book sales, be willing and prepared to make change. At the time of this writing, most of the common coin-op machines accept only coins and small bills. If you can find a solution that puts the keys to the coin box in your hands rather than in those of an external vendor, seize it; this will allow you to clear so many of the jams and errors that plague these things yourself instead of waiting for someone to come to your rescue.

Another aspect to consider about the experience of using these technologies at libraries is how access to them is granted. Do patrons need to log in to computer stations or use their library card bar codes to identify and claim a print job? Are there express stations where visitors or people in a hurry can bypass such steps? Is there actually a good reason for having the bar code log-in system in place, or does it prevent people from accessing the internet when they need to and might not have another way of doing so? Often, these bar code log-in systems are tied to age group information on a patron's library card to ensure, for example, that children's room computers are being used by children. Do you *need* to apply the same logic to the adult stations? A 2016 post to the Electronic Frontier Foundation's blog suggests that the use of patron bar codes as a log-in credential undermines users' privacy.[10]

This isn't to say there aren't use cases for doing these things; this is just an encouragement to think about the underlying reasoning instead of just defaulting to how it's always been done. It's also good to think such things over before replacing your current system with a new one. Think about the nuts and bolts of what your patrons really need, and err on the side of simplicity. Try to keep services consistent too; for example, don't offer guest passes to the computers in one branch but not another. The experience of using these technologies can be frustrating enough without throwing in the extra complication of inconsistent policies and uneven expectations.

LIBRARY WEBSITE AND SOCIAL MEDIA

Callan once worked as a web designer for hair salons and spas in the northeastern region of the United States. This was around the advent of Web 2.0, when businesses that hadn't gotten online yet were enticed by social media to bolster their advertising to new clients. When working with salon and spa owners, Callan found they would often gush about their stylists and how they wanted pages with photos and biographies for everyone on the staff. Some of them would write lengthy descriptions of even the most basic boilerplate services, like a pedicure or a bang trim. She had to gently remind them that customers weren't coming to their sites to read about the life story of the person who'd be doing their eyebrow threading; they were looking for hours, directions, and pricing, and not much else.

Consider this: What are patrons trying to do on your website? You can find out about this a little more empirically if you want to test your assumptions. Web analytics tools like Google Analytics and Matomo can quickly generate a list of your most visited pages. You can also do short surveys with your patrons to ask them directly. Most libraries will see a list of most visited pages that includes at least some of the following:

- hours
- directions
- catalog/resource access
- contact information
- events
- borrowing policies/loan or fine information

This varies between different types of libraries, as some pages and services just aren't relevant in certain settings; for instance, public libraries will often see youth services pages near the top, whereas academic libraries will see a lot of clicks on database and journal access.

Once you have a sense of what people are trying to do on your site, you can dig into whether or not they're able to do it. Aaron Schmidt and Amanda Etches describe a trinity of good UX; the first element is usability.[11] To be usable, a site needs to scale down and be accessible on every device, mobile and screen reader friendly (this is called responsive design). It needs to use balanced design elements and reduce visual clutter; it should be organized with a navigation menu that empowers people to find what they're after by following a logical series of steps. This is closely aligned with usefulness; the site cannot be useful if it's not usable. The goal of virtually every library website is to get patrons to the information they need from or about the library, and the site is useful only if it succeeds in doing that. Also at the core of usability and usefulness is accessibility.

Last, whether or not something is desirable depends on whether it's useful and usable, but it also has a lot to do with aesthetics. Font choices should be modern, consistent, and readable. Colors should follow established brand guidelines (time to pull those together if you don't have them yet!). Clues like hovering color changes or underlining should be used as gentle signposts along the way to the right track. This is another wheel we don't need to reinvent. The web is filled with beautifully designed sites. Steal inspiration from big companies that have whole graphic design departments and UX researchers; adapt their fonts, color choices, language, and log-in boxes. Using standard design elements reduces cognitive load, meaning there's less to bog people down and distract them as they're on the information hunt.

Don't forget, too, that you aren't beholden to the website as a singular platform for publishing content. You've got an array of social media options at your fingertips, and many applications exist to help you manage posting to more than one of them at once. Rather than listing out the options of the day and the types of communication each one seems best suited for, we are going to acknowledge that both of these factors are subject to rapid change and suggest instead that you do some homework today—whenever that day might be—on what's working well in other libraries and businesses.

Focus on crafting the message first and then choosing the right medium for it. If you want to do a behind-the-scenes post about what it's like to work at the library, think about what's more likely to draw people in: a video of opening a box of new books or listing out the titles in an update with text and no images. Play to your strengths and what people on your staff have the passion and time to sustainably create. If you have people who want to, and can, consistently write blog posts for your website, let them do it, but don't force it if the interest isn't there. And if the blog posts are getting one page view every six months but your social media posts are netting hundreds of clicks and "people reached," it might be time to pull the plug on the blog and consider different forms of outreach. E-mail newsletters aren't a new concept, but they have seen a resurgence among online communication methods because they come to you versus expecting you—busy you, with all your shiny social media accounts and other online pastimes—to come to them.

LIBRARY IT TEAMS AND COMMUNICATION

Before we start talking about communication, we need to talk about your team. Do you have one? If not, can you make one? You might be a team of one, but that manifests itself in different ways. Some librarians are truly going it alone, and if that's you, you have our sympathy and respect. More often than not, one-person teams have colleagues who just aren't doing the exact same work, perhaps because their job descriptions don't include it or because they don't think they're capable. If that's your situation and you're the solo tech person, try starting a tech committee. This could be as simple as a monthly meeting during which you run your upcoming goals past a subset of your colleagues and solicit their feedback; ideally, they'll share their ideas with you too.

You can also empower your colleagues to help you with tasks that are traditionally left for tech staff to do but don't require special expertise, like installing certain kinds of updates or basic troubleshooting. If you find your colleagues are hesitant to take part in this work, it may be because of bad past experiences they've had with prior technologists in your position or at other jobs or because of underlying insecurities they feel about technology in general. Do your best to alleviate these fears by being kind and patient, offering hands-on guidance, and expressing your gratitude to people for trying.

Consider a Ticketing System

If you do have an internal library IT team or a group of staff members who help out with tech issues, if you haven't yet, please stop communicating through e-mail alone. Ticketing systems will restore hope where there has been only sorrow, and they can help as well with other communication bottlenecks in the library, tech-related or otherwise. It's also ideal to have some form of real-time conversation, be it a text message thread, a chat service (e.g., Google Hangouts), or a workplace messenger platform (e.g., Slack). With this combination, your IT folks will always know who's dealing with what and when; they'll know what fires need putting out right away and which ones have been put out already. Trying to manage requests for help via e-mail alone is a square peg–round hole situation; there's no great way to mark a task as completed or pending, you can easily wind up with one person receiving all of the requests for support, or you'll have senders replying all to the whole team about half the time, meaning no one will be on the same page.

Help Desk and Ticketing Systems

Rival help desk and ticketing solutions abound. We're a big fan of library software company Springshare's LibAnswers, which boasts a reasonable price tag and includes add-ons like the ability to publish FAQs in a publicly searchable knowledge base as well as text and chat reference services. Ticketing versus e-mail lets you see who has responded to a request for support and whether an issue is closed (i.e., fixed) or pending. Tickets can be assigned to certain members of your team with particular expertise. They can be tagged with common topics, allowing you to identify trends in what people are most often asking about. Ticketing gives you organization and analysis that goes way beyond what you could pull off with your e-mail inbox.

How does ticketing relate to user experience? On the one hand, staff get their questions answered more quickly and more reliably, because they're not prone to slipping through the e-mail cracks. Most of the tickets they're opening probably have to do with helping patrons do something, like printing or accessing the internet. Faster answers for staff means faster answers for patrons. It's simple enough, too, to use a service like LibAnswers to field questions both internally and externally by using different queues for different types of questions. At one of her past libraries, Callan implemented an IT-specific queue available to only staff and a queue connected to a generic Contact Us form on the library's homepage that made it a cinch to route any kind of question to the person on staff who could best answer it. Staff also took advantage of LibAnswers' built-in chat service to provide chat reference during certain busy hours each day. This improved service by leaps and bounds over sending e-mail to a single mailbox monitored by only one person.

Make Friends with the External IT Team

Chances are you're going to be working with some sort of external IT department, whether or not you have your own library tech folks in-house. This could be an academic or company-wide IT team or a separate town department. Chances are also good that this group of nonlibrary IT workers is not going to really get what you're doing, especially if the library hasn't done much to branch out in their direction before, whether it's to ask for help or to get in lockstep with other departments in terms of equipment and management.

We mentioned the drawbacks of silos earlier. Libraries suffer when they go without the help of their colleagues in town, city, or campus IT departments. Library workers don't often have the resources to keep on top of security, bandwidth, upkeep, and other issues and needs, and we should try not to force this responsibility on them. While it's smart and advisable to expect librarians to beef up their patron-centered tech knowledge—meaning things like using e-books and e-readers, troubleshooting basic computing and printing issues, and understanding ILSs and catalogs thoroughly to be able to adeptly resolve common problems—it's not reasonable to expect them to do all of that and *also* program the Cisco network switches in the server room or rattle off the differences between wireless protocols. Put another way, IT skills like network administration should ideally remain the domain of IT professionals; library tech folks should focus on library-specific tech and be able to explain it to general IT staff.

Of course, this requires an interest in and the willingness to work together on the part of nonlibrary IT staff as well, and inspiring that can be easier said than done. If you're struggling with this in your own setting, whether you're working in a public, academic, or another type of library, consider the following before you assume they're just being unreasonable:

- They may not have had any relationship with the library previously.
- They may not understand what is special or different about library technology. That can take a couple distinct forms: They might have no idea what RFID pads are (and they almost certainly don't know how they work, which we're not saying to be snobby; they're just something that's very library). They might understand but not fully grasp what it means to have to manage both staff- and public-facing technologies; for instance, they might not realize that public computer stations experience a degree of wear and tear that isn't comparable to town accountants clacking away on their keyboards in their private offices.
- The library might have reached out to the external IT department only when it was trying to avert or react to a crisis, as opposed to engaging in proactive or collaborative outreach. No one likes this; it's a bit like not texting a friend for a year until you want to ask for a ride to the airport.

- The library might be unaware of or not following guidelines or rules that have been enforced with other departments. For example, many IT departments have pretty strict schedules for cycling new equipment in and out (like in the form of multiyear leases or purchasing cycles). They also usually don't want other departments buying things that connect to their network without consulting them first.

The bottom line here is that you need to talk to your external IT staff. You need to get on the same page about expectations for who's doing what and make sure that any guidelines that you should be following are clearly articulated and explained.

The end goal for an initial meeting with external IT staff should be unifying your tech plans and goals with theirs (and the rest of the town, campus, or company). Because there's nothing indicating technology will be *less* of a part of our jobs in the future, we have to try to sustainably plan for what's to come, and the reality is that most libraries don't have the people, knowledge, or time to be able to handle all their technology needs on their own. Instead, we should zero in on what is specific to us (circulation equipment and software) and what people are coming to us for (public computers and printers; general tech help). By relying on and clearly communicating with our external IT staff, we can refocus ourselves on customer service and individualized help. If our external IT team is ready and willing to assist with our infrastructural needs, we can free up time and dollars spent on trying to do that ourselves. We can better equip our staff and, as a direct result, better serve our patrons.

MAKERSPACES

In their early days, makerspaces looked like a passing craze, but they have endured the test of time in libraries. Even 3-D printers aren't weird novelties anymore; they're used in manufacturing, medicine, and many other fields. Plotters that can quickly cut designs out of vinyl, card stock, and fabric are helping people create everything from new fashions (and small businesses) to homemade gifts to custom signage for public spaces. The more analog offerings of these spaces, like sewing machines and other crafting materials, remain popular as well. Librarians have championed the unique pedagogical value of makerspaces, describing them as places where new types of literacy can be explored and unexpected collaborations can take root. Some have argued that as daily life grows more and more digital and abstract, the urge to physically manipulate and create in some more tangible way grows too. During the COVID-19 crisis in 2020, library makerspaces joined in the effort to manufacture medical masks, face shields, and other personal protective equipment when the United States began running out of supplies.

A library's makerspace, if it chooses to have one at all, should be guided by what patrons want, what they'll actually use, and what is reasonable to expect library staff to learn how to operate. That means, like just about everything else we've mentioned in this book, they need to be customized for their communities. We have found that a lot of librarians know their patrons want a makerspace but get stuck on how to provide one. They often are intimidated by the very term itself. It sounds flashy and modern and full of expensive gadgets. That leads to fears and budgetary concerns about having to buy new furniture and fixtures, adding to other feelings of nervousness around needing to know how to use everything in the space.

The good news is you don't need that glass-enclosed laboratory full of glinting steel bar stools, huge flat-screen TVs, and brand-new modular tables you might have spotted in a nearby library. We know of libraries that can spare only a book truck to host their making tools but still get tons of interest in them. Think instead about how to make people feel welcome and *invited* to make. Try to repurpose an underutilized area that's still accessible, well lit, and preferably well ventilated. Advertise your events and tools to groups in multiple languages and scope programming to different age and skill levels. If you're pressed for space, go with a more mobile option. It's best to start small to test out the interest, in terms of both deciding what tools and equipment to buy and knowing what kind of materials budget might be required for consumables (e.g., 3-D printer filament, wood sheets for laser cutting, rolls of vinyl).

How to Make a Makerspace

A decent combination of tools for a starter makerspace would be a small, low-cost 3-D printer; a sewing machine or two; a portable vinyl/paper plotter or two; and a button maker (no, seriously, kids and teens *adore* these things). If you have a little more to spend, there are some truly magical laser cutters on the market at the time of this writing. These machines can cut through and engrave wood, acrylic, card stock, and more. As with every other technology in the library, focus on user needs and desires. Patrons of all ages like to take things home with them and to make gifts or decorations, so it's smart to focus on relatively simple fabrication tools. They're also looking for a place to try things out that they might never invest in or have the space for at home, like 3-D printers and laser cutters.

Some patrons might seek you out for more complex projects, like the fellow we met at a nearby makerspace who builds his own mandolins and guitars with pieces he laser cuts at the library. If you're lucky, you might be able to ask some of these more advanced makers to volunteer to teach classes in your space. Many librarians with successful makerspaces will tell you with some awe about the makers who came out of nowhere to offer their time and skills to the community. If you're worried about staffing or your team's expertise or interest in these tools, try to harvest the passion of these members of the public. And last but not least, busy as you might be, give yourself the chance to have fun making yourself. You might find a new hobby, and you'll get to see why your patrons are so jazzed up about having access to these tools.

CODING SKILLS

In the United States, we hear quite a bit about the lack of skilled workers in computer science and information technology. There has been a response in the corporate sector, including from companies such as Google that have the resources to campaign for and support building those missing skills among members of the workforce. Though the ethics around partnerships with giants of surveillance capitalism (see the final section of this chapter) make us queasy, it still bears mentioning that Google has offered grants to public libraries and conducted its Grow with Google training workshops at them as well.[12] Some Google-supported grants have focused on enhancing computational literacy skills to prime young patrons for jobs in software design and engineering.[13] To keep up with these needs, libraries have partnered with or applied for money from these companies, hosted community educators such as Girls Who Code groups, or organized their own coding programs for patrons of all ages (particularly children and teens).

Does that mean you need to hire a crack team of experts who can write you custom software or at least a custom curriculum for coding camps? Do you need people with skills sections on their résumés that are stuffed with abbreviations that you might not even recognize? The short answer is no. The longer answer is this: although it's good to have a team with as many types of skill sets as you can get your hands on, you're not likely to find computer science or engineering majors looking to work at library-level salaries. You also cannot expect your technology or reference staff, or yourself, to have every single type of tech ability under the sun. Running coding programs for patrons is a popular activity that serves a real need in society, but you can rely on preexisting resources, community partners, or staff members who might just have a passion for this stuff.

If you're hiring for someone to work in a tech-centric library role, pay more attention to curiosity and approachability than to specific coding languages. Languages come and go in popularity and utility. Also, the reality of many library jobs—especially in public libraries—is that coding is a pretty small component of the work compared with the time spent helping people use existing hardware and software. We've heard about coding programs for kids that encourage the softer skills of collaboration, constructive criticism, and finding multiple solutions to a given problem. Rather than hunting for or aspiring to be a unicorn, try to find candidates for jobs or build your own skills with these important aspects in mind.

Library Research and Development

Librarianship as a whole definitely needs to entice computer scientists and engineers to work with us on, well, everything. As the lack of usability of various library-specific technologies shows, we've missed out on advancements in user experience and aesthetics that have reshaped so many other aspects of modern life. We have clung to many aging standards, practices, and tools because alternatives haven't really been presented to us. Our systems for inventory control, online resource access, print vending, and many other key tasks are creaky and stale. Libraries need research and development.

How might we make that happen? Some groups are attempting to serve this role, like the Metropolitan New York Library Council (METRO) in New York City, which is currently working on developing noncorporate approaches to digitizing and preserving cultural resources.* Library-themed hackathons are sporadically hosted at universities or local nonprofits. We can also advocate for ourselves in unconventional spaces, like the Interactive Tracks at the South by Southwest (SXSW) Conference, and with people working in tech across a constellation of industries from health care to robotics who might have never even considered us as potential clients. Libraries, like Austin Central Library down the street from SXSW, have offered display space to innovators looking to show off or gather feedback about their new gadgets and programs. Much more needs to be done, and it all starts with us stepping beyond our professional comfort zone and finding unlikely allies in the world beyond Libraryland.

* METRO, "Software Services," https://metro.org/software/; see also Archipelago Commons at http://archipelago.nyc.

CIRCULATING TECHNOLOGY

In addition to providing the space for people to play and experiment with new technology, libraries are also giving patrons a chance to take those technologies home. They're circulating everything from streaming sticks to video game consoles to electricity monitors to kitchen gadgets. They're also making available for in-house use an increasing number of tech amenities, like laptops and charging cables.

Similar to starting a simple makerspace, if you've identified a desire for a circulating tech collection, you should start small. The most obvious and universally helpful item is phone-charging tech, whether you get standard charging cables or, to avoid people walking off with them, you buy a docking station with battery packs that are useless without the dock. Beyond that, you should respond to needs as you see them popping up. For instance, if you're frantically trying to accommodate users on public desktop computers, circulating cheap laptops could be a low-impact way to bolster your fleet. If patrons want to watch shows on streaming services that aren't available on physical media yet (or won't ever be), offer streaming tools for them to borrow so they can decide if the tools are worth the cost to own them. iPads and other tablets can be very popular as well, especially if you load them up with apps that patrons might want to try. These devices offer a range of helpful tech for parents, patrons who need assistive technology, and educators.

The biggest headache with circulating most technologies is that they haven't been designed for a library's use case, particularly in the realm of account and device management. Apple provides device management options, but they're a little too high-octane for most library situations. With iPads, newer video consoles, and streaming tech, you'll need to create accounts to help you manage the devices. Some patrons might choose to sign in with their own accounts, and it's generally not worth the effort to prevent them from doing so, but most people who borrow these items will be starting from scratch. Learn what you can about the easiest solutions for resetting these devices, which staff should do every time they're returned to the library for the sake of patron privacy. You'll also need to look into ways to lock down certain features for simplifying device management, like disabling buying new apps or the deletion of ones you want to be sure to keep. Approaches to device management are clunky and inconsistent, and many tech providers change their systems often (we're looking at you, Apple), so keep in mind that the device management side of things will impact the amount of time and effort you have to invest in a collection of borrowable tech. The good news is that this is another case of not having to reinvent the wheel. Be sure to check with nearby libraries that are already circulating these items to ask if you can copy their device management strategies.

Another caveat with these collections is that they tend to have a short shelf life, not only because they're more prone to damage or missing pieces than are more traditional materials. They get outdated quickly or other technologies beat them at their own game. Think about a collection of high-end digital cameras, for instance. Before smartphones began beefing up their cameras and offering more professional-grade features, an entry-level DSLR (digital single-lens reflex) camera would have made excellent library-of-things material. But now that many phones can take photos that rival the quality of a stand-alone camera, it might make more sense to invest in cell phone gimbals or phone-attachable microphones that cost less and could attract more interest through their convenience and simplicity. If you don't know which option would be better for your patrons, don't forget that you can just *ask them*.

Beware of Zip Tie Fixes

Previously, we mentioned the zip ties binding together clusters of ten-year-old cables in a dusty tangle beneath a circulation desk. Zip tie fixes will address a problem today (keeping cables neat) but can be more trouble than they're worth a little later down the road. An example of this happened a few years ago, when Google offered trials of its free G Suite for Education management product to public libraries. Libraries that took advantage of the free trial used it to set up e-mail addresses on custom domains and benefited from its other services, but their eligibility for the free version was eventually rescinded. They then had to decide between paying big bucks as a government client or leaving what they'd set up in their accounts to fester in oblivion.

Another common zip tie fix comes in the form of a one-time grant or gift of a certain technology or service to the library that doesn't get factored into a replacement cycle or a standing budgetary increase. A risk that's probably more often seen in academic libraries, but can happen anywhere, arises when a student or staff member develops a custom tool or program to complete a task but then leaves and takes their knowledge of and ability to support it with them. Sometimes, for the sake of stability, choosing the less interesting and more traditional route is safer; it can even lead to more creativity down the road as time spent doing basic triage on custom solutions is freed up for different kinds of exploration.

ACCESSIBILITY AND INCLUSIVE DESIGN IN TECHNOLOGY

Accessibility as we define it in this book refers to the design of products, devices, services, or environments so as to be usable by people with differing abilities. Inclusive design, sometimes called universal design, is the practice of creating products that are usable by people with the widest possible range of abilities, operating within the widest possible range of situations.[14]

Accessibility and inclusive design have a shared history, as described by the Institute for Human Centered Design (IHCD), stemming from legal efforts to develop standards for making buildings and streets more wheelchair accessible. "It had become clear that many other people benefitted from the standards despite that narrow focus," the IHCD writes.[15] "Curb cuts, ramps and accessible vertical access made wheeled luggage the rational choice for everyone. Few people used wheelchairs but ten times that number had difficulty walking." The need for accessibility for some led to designs that benefit us all. Technology offers tons of examples of this, from voice-activated personal digital assistants to responsive design and browser reader modes that make it much easier to resize and view websites on smartphones.

Libraries should strive for inclusive design of their websites and other tech offerings. Websites should be kept simple and screen reader friendly, using contrasting colors and user-friendly font choices. As mentioned in the section on library websites, they also need to be responsive; this is absolutely essential, not a nice-to-have, in the 2020s. If you're not sure about the accessibility of your website or a certain element within it, such as a slider or carousel that reduces page size by allowing side scrolling through blocks of content, many resources on the web can help you find out. Follow guidelines for accessible online design, such as the latest standards from the World Wide Web

Consortium (W3C), and use the evaluation tools provided on the W3C's "Web Accessibility Evaluation Tools List."[16] None of this can substitute for consulting people who depend on screen readers or other assistive technologies when you're designing services for them. Ask your patrons and staff members to help you find people to consult or turn to a state or national organization that works with folks with visual impairments.

These guidelines go beyond making sure your site meets the baseline criteria—that you've provided alternative text for all of your photos, for example—and ask that you design the whole thing to make sense on a more structural level. One of the W3C's success criteria is that sites are designed with a meaningful sequence of information: "When the sequence in which content is presented affects its meaning, a correct reading sequence can be programmatically determined."[17] This means that a given page should be designed so that assistive technologies can help users navigate the order of the content without leaving them confused. To make that happen, you might need to rethink a creative or unconventional layout for a given page. Your users must always come first over unique design.

Moving beyond websites, many library technologies need accessibility improvements, and like it or not, it's on us to pressure vendors to make those changes. Most public computer systems offer a large-print option, which is a step in the right direction. Some of these same systems, however, have changed the look and feel of their desktops and toolbars to the point where the visual language is confusing to many patrons. Keep this in mind when assessing self-checkout options. It is good if they offer language choices other than English, but don't stop there: make sure they offer a voice-controlled option and have a universally accessible touch screen height. For the sake of our staff as well as our patrons, our checkout and inventory control systems could benefit from adjustable font sizes. We can make some middle-of-the-road fixes, like purchasing technology that specifically focuses on accessibility and showing patrons how to get the most out of it.

Consider acquiring peripherals like high-contrast keyboards and mice with large trackballs that can be controlled with motions other than fine motor skills of the hand; these could be for library use only or part of a circulating technology collection. Many libraries offer accessibility toolkits, including low-vision signature guides to help patrons sign their library cards, checks, and other forms as well as magnifying sheets for assistance with viewing maps or other large documents. An inexpensive solution for most libraries is screen-enlarging software like ZoomText; there are also some open source alternatives to the JAWS screen reader available online at the time of this writing.

Don't stop there and don't avoid asking for money for these services if you need it. Libraries have a tendency to do things cheaply by default; just think of all the conference programs you've gone to called "How to Do [Insert Important Task Here] on a Shoestring Budget." Hopefully, the powers that be will agree with you that it's a critical part of your operating budget to help everyone who comes your way, regardless of their abilities. You should also explain that it's worth paying for the reliability and familiarity of tools that your patrons are likely using already. If the funds truly can't come from local donations, consider options for partnering with local schools, municipal groups like a Council on Aging, Lions Clubs, Braille and talking book libraries, or other community-oriented nonprofits. Apply for grants at the state or national level. Try to push the envelope beyond just providing text magnifiers by acquiring funds for a circulating tablet program that includes a budget for assistive apps to try.

We're really excited about an organization called Makers Making Change, a program that works to connect volunteer makers with people in need of assistive technology. On its website (www.makersmakingchange.com), the organization offers a library of different project plans and design files for 3-D printing, soldering, and assembling components into affordable assistive devices. Products include cutlery support for folks with motor skill issues, gaming pads that can be played using different parts of the body or gestures, signature guides, and LipSync, a mouth-controlled device used to operate touch screens. If you have a makerspace, consider hosting an accessibility hackathon during which you use the design files provided by Makers Making Change. You could work on your own local needs as well. One library near us used a 3-D printer to create a dog paw–friendly cover for the buttons used to automatically open their accessible doors, making it easier for service animals to help their owners. Hacking accessibility is a great way to use your gadgets for good.

AUTOMATION, ARTIFICIAL INTELLIGENCE, PRIVACY, AND SURVEILLANCE

Callan went to a conference talk in the fall of 2019 during which the speaker mused about the replacement of librarians with robots, citing examples ranging from the worker bee–style book trucks of the Helsinki Library in Finland to an artificially intelligent reference robot named Hugh at the University of Aberystwyth in Wales. It's hard to imagine a future where a library staff position is given to an expensive robot instead of just being outright eliminated, especially as we're watching unprecedented numbers of our colleagues being laid off and furloughed as a response to the financial devastation caused by COVID-19, but it's useful, if worrisome, to think about where automation can help us in our work as well as how it will impact society.

Automated materials handlers, or book sorters, are not as humanoid as the aforementioned robots, but they stand to change workflows in the library, likely for the better. We should be careful not to position these developments as cutting staffing costs but argue instead that they free up staff to work on other tasks that robots aren't nearly as good for, like providing excellent customer service and running interesting new events. Many busy librarians—the frontline circulation staff in particular—would remain just as busy even if they weren't frantically checking items in and reshelving them.

ALA's Center for the Future of Libraries cautions us that the job displacement artificial intelligence (AI) may cause could prove more disruptive than that seen during traditional economic slowdowns. To keep one step ahead of AI, workers will need specialized knowledge and applied skills. "The new workforce development demands will likely require higher-order critical, creative, and innovative thinking as well as emotional engagement," notes the center's 2019 report, "placing a greater value on the quality of thinking, listening, relating, collaborating, and learning."[18]

Questions of algorithmic bias and literacy also beg for libraries' attention when there aren't many, or any, alternative venues for educating the public about these new opportunities and threats. On a 2018 episode of the podcast *At Liberty*, from the American Civil Liberties Union (ACLU), Meredith Whittaker, an expert on digital privacy and security issues, explains that algorithms require

> data that, given the nature of space-time, was created in the past. And this data necessarily reflects the patterns of discrimination, of oppression, the patterns of life as it is. . . . AI systems often not only replicate, but in some senses can amplify and mask existing patterns of oppression and discrimination.[19]

The architects of these algorithms, given the predominantly white and male membership of the tech companies that employ them, are not exactly shining examples of diversity themselves.

Facial recognition technology is one of the most alarming and problematic examples of algorithmic bias. As of early 2020, the ACLU of Massachusetts is still hard at work on efforts to halt adoption of these tools in a campaign called Press Pause on Face Surveillance. In a fact sheet, the organization cites numerous examples of misidentification and disproportionate inaccuracies among certain races and genders, particularly black women. The authors write, "Most software is trained on datasets that overwhelmingly represent white men, and then deployed on datasets that often disproportionately represent Black men (e.g. mugshot databases)."[20]

In her book the *Age of Surveillance Capitalism*, Shoshana Zuboff warns of the power today's tech giants yield over the general public with their shadowy systems of making money off our behavior; she suggests that companies like Amazon, Facebook, and Google are aiming to automate *us*, not stopping at just the collection of our information.[21] In an interview with *The Guardian* about her book, Zuboff refers to a data scientist who described it to her this way: "We can engineer the context around a particular behaviour and force change that way. . . . We are learning how to write the music, and then we let the music make them dance."[22]

Surveillance is far more pervasive and dangerous than what the current social media giants are making their millions off of. In her book *Dark Matters: On the Blackness of Surveillance*, Simone Browne describes how surveillance has roots in slavery. She shows how the design of slave ships, the branding of slaves, and laws aimed at controlling Black and indigenous peoples in the eighteenth century are the precursors of today's biometrics and emotion-reading technologies. Her examples also reflect the power and threat of algorithmic bias:

> You have a large push into affective computing technologies, the kind of machine reading of emotions being used at airports, for example, in Israel, which monitor people for blood pressure, for sweat and for changes in their voice, and then assign a threat category or score to them. These kinds of affective computing technologies amp up the role of affect, which, as we know, is something that is socially constructed. This gets us to think about: Who gets marked as "angry" prior to any reaction? [T]his harkens back to the controlling images of the "angry Black woman" and the "threatening Black man."[23]

When considering how surveillance impacts library patrons, we should acknowledge that marginalized people are the most endangered by this technological overreach. It's important for us to stay true to our deeply held professional ethics of patron privacy and to educate our communities about the impacts of surveillance tech. Similarly, our nonwhite patrons are at disproportionate risk from other practices, like calling the police to respond to library incidents. Libraries are trusted resources in their communities. They should work to foster and encourage that trust by divesting from practices known to harm their most vulnerable patrons. We offer some suggestions on how libraries might do this work later in the chapter.

Zuboff also focuses on what she calls the division of learning, a shift away from the traditional division of labor in the workplace.[24] The division of learning arises when workers, impacted by rapid technological shifts such as increasing automation, experience unequal opportunities and encouragement for adapting to changing roles, tasks, and responsibilities. This feeds back into the Center for the Future of Libraries' prediction that libraries will play a role in helping displaced workers—those on the wrong side of the division of learning—find a way to shore up their higher-order thinking skills or explore new avenues for employment.[25]

Libraries act in defiance of a time when personal data is hoovered up and, as Zuboff has described it, rendered into "behavioral surplus" that gets used to build prediction products about us all.[26] We (mostly) don't share the little data we collect, and the scant few systems that attempt to make predictions to patrons are entirely opt-in features. There's no secret mission to automate our patrons' behavior; the very notion of that contradicts our professional ethics and commitment to intellectual freedom. We're rebels, not Luddites, in the age of surveillance capitalism, as libraries are built on a foundation of open information sharing and user privacy. In his 2003 book the *Ultimate Digital Library*, mentioned in the introduction, Andrew K. Pace presciently calls for librarians to push vendors harder and to critically evaluate the products and content they're being sold.[27]

"User education just might be the best weapon libraries have to compete with duplicitous, disingenuous, monopolistic, and parasitic Internet businesses."[28] Pace wrote that—*in 2003*. We could easily say the same thing about the architects of the behavior-monitoring, ad revenue-driven web we have today. Reading Pace's section on eroding expectations of privacy is a bit like seeing a blurry premonition of the surveilled society we live in today. Near the end of the book, he writes, "Libraries have the distinct advantage of ultimately being able to ignore the bottom line. . . . It is not that information wants to be free; librarians want information to be valuable."[29] The giants of surveillance capitalism have their own definition of and parameters for the value of information, and they have benefited handsomely from the advantages they've given themselves.

Librarians, well equipped as we are with our ethics and professional goals, should act as a counterweight to these companies, as it's unclear who else might rein them in. We have many options for doing this work, whether it's hosting book clubs and author talks about these topics, offering digital self-defense courses, cosigning support for legislation as part of our state-level member organizations, or performing direct forms of advocacy alongside ideological allies such as the ACLU and Electronic Frontier Foundation. The Library Freedom Project (LFP), founded in 2015, is an organization focused on helping library workers develop "skills necessary to turn [these] ideals into action."[30] (See figure 4.2.) Callan was a cohort member of the third Library Freedom Institute, an LFP partnership with New York University to provide an immersive short course on privacy rights and libraries' role in fighting surveillance, during the COVID-19 crisis. The curriculum pivoted to cover important digital privacy issues that arose in the pandemic, such as the rapid shift to online instruction and the conversation around temperature tracking and other health monitoring.

FIGURE 4.2

Focusing on surveillance technology and its disproportionate impacts on marginalized people, the Library Freedom Project trains and supports library workers to become vocal community advocates for privacy.

So much more could be said on the topic of surveillance capitalism and how patron privacy is at risk from unprecedented corporate overreach, but that's beyond the scope of this book. For our purposes, let's leave it here: Artificial intelligence, automation, and surveillance are all impacting libraries, whether or not librarians are ultimately replaced by robots. We have a critical role to play in fostering discussions and understanding about the technologies at the forefront of disrupting our workplaces and society as a whole. Our libraries are hubs for connection that offer resources to community members in need of job searching, application, or skill-building assistance. We and our libraries also have traits that cannot simply be automated away: the serendipity of browsing our shelves and the comfort of storytime; the human presence in help with a technology issue; the trust patrons place in us; our ability to doggedly explore the twists and turns of a research question that a machine may not fully understand; the very existence of our space.

NOTES

1. Massachusetts Board of Library Commissioners, "Electronic Services: 2018 Report," https://mblc.state.ma.us/programs-and-support/library-statistics/files/data/2018/2018_Electronic_Services.xlsx.
2. Isimon, "These Closed Libraries Are Still Providing Free Wi-Fi," I Love Libraries, an initiative of the American Library Association, March 25, 2020, www.ilovelibraries.org/article/these-closed-libraries-are-still-providing-free-wi-fi.
3. "Kearney Public Library Parking Lot Gets WiFi," Kearney Hub, April 1, 2020, www.kearneyhub.com/news/local/kearney-public-library-parking-lot-gets-wifi/article_a62a1592-7431-11ea-af03-47dc05a89239.html.
4. Pew Research Center, "Americans and Digital Knowledge," Internet and Technology, October 9, 2019, www.pewresearch.org/internet/2019/10/09/americans-and-digital-knowledge/.
5. Microsoft Dynamics 365, "2018 State of Global Customer Service Report," Microsoft, https://info.microsoft.com/ww-landing-State-of-Global-Customer-Service-Report-Microsoft-Dynamics-365-eBook.html?lcid=en-us.
6. Microsoft Dynamics 365, "2018 Customer Service Report," 14.
7. Microsoft Dynamics 365, "2018 Customer Service Report," 26.
8. Microsoft Dynamics 365, "2018 Customer Service Report," 42.
9. "Episode 146: Summer Hotline," Reply All (podcast), July 25, 2019, www.stitcher.com/podcast/gimlet/reply-all/e/62792698.
10. Gennie Gebhart and Kerry Sheehan, "Librarians, Act Now to Protect Your Users (Before It's Too Late)," Electronic Frontier Foundation blog, December 5, 2016, www.eff.org/deeplinks/2016/12/librarians-act-now-protect-your-users-its-too-late.
11. Aaron Schmidt and Amanda Etches, Useful, Usable, Desirable: Applying User Experience Design to your Library (Chicago: ALA Editions, 2014).

12. Public Library Association, "Libraries Lead with Digital Skills," American Library Association, www.ala.org/pla/initiatives/google.

13. Libraries Ready to Code, "Digital Skills Programs Minigrants," American Library Association, www.ala.org/tools/readytocode/minigrant.

14. Rosemarie Rossetti, "The Seven Principles of Universal Design," *Action Magazine*, December 2006, www.udll.com/media-room/articles/the-seven-principles-of -universal-design/.

15. Institute for Human Centered Design, "History," www.humancentereddesign .org/inclusive-design/history/.

16. W3C, *Web Content Accessibility Guidelines (WCAG) 2.1* (W3C Recommendation, June 5, 2018), www.w3.org/TR/WCAG21/; W3C, "Web Accessibility Evaluation Tools List," updated March 2016, www.w3.org/WAI/ER/tools/.

17. W3C, *Web Content Accessibility Guidelines*, Success Criterion 1.3.2 Meaningful Sequence.

18. Center for the Future of Libraries, "Artificial Intelligence," American Library Association, February 4, 2019, www.ala.org/tools/future/trends/ artificialintelligence.

19. American Civil Liberties Union (ACLU), "How to Fight an Algorithm," *At Liberty* (podcast), episode 7, August 2, 2018, www.aclu.org/podcast/ how-fight-algorithm-ep-7.

20. ACLU Massachusetts, "Face Surveillance and Racial Bias" (Press Pause on Face Surveillance fact sheet), www.aclum.org/sites/default/files/field_documents/ presspause_face_surveillance_and_race.pdf.

21. Shoshana Zuboff, *The Age of Surveillance Capitalism* (New York: Public Affairs, 2019).

22. John Naughton, "'The Goal Is to Automate Us': Welcome to the Age of Surveillance Capitalism," *The Guardian*, January 20, 2019, www.theguardian .com/technology/2019/jan/20/shoshana-zuboff-age-of-surveillance-capitalism -google-facebook.

23. Claudio Garcia-Rojas, "The Surveillance of Blackness: From the Trans-Atlantic Slave Trade to Contemporary Surveillance Technologies," *Truthout*, March 3, 2016, https://truthout.org/articles/the-surveillance-of-blackness -from-the-slave-trade-to-the-police/.

24. Zuboff, *Age of Surveillance Capitalism*.

25. Center for the Future of Libraries, "Artificial Intelligence."

26. Lance Farrell, "Shoshana Zuboff: Rendering Reality and Cash Cows," *Science Node*, October 17, 2017, https://sciencenode.org/feature/shoshana-zuboff, -part-two-rendering-reality.php.

27. Andrew K. Pace, *The Ultimate Digital Library* (Chicago: ALA Editions, 2003).

28. Pace, *Ultimate Digital Library*, 113.

29. Pace, *Ultimate Digital Library*, 135.

30. Library Freedom Project, "What Does Library Freedom Project Do?," https:// libraryfreedom.org.

5
Physical Spaces

So far we've mostly been talking about technology, ground zero for UX principles. Your building and everything in it can be vastly improved with these techniques too. They can be applied whether you are contemplating a brand-new facility, a refresh or reconfiguration, or just a few tweaks in layout.

COLLECTIONS

Remember the five laws of library science by S. R. Ranganathan?

1. Books are for use.
2. Every person his or her book.
3. Every book its reader.
4. Save the time of the reader.
5. A library is a growing organism.[1]

There is no topic in libraries more rife with speculation than physical collections. What should be purchased? What should be retained? What size collection should a particular library have? How aggressively should the collection be weeded? What should be collected in print and what is better addressed with digital resources?

For physical collections (and the space required to house them), the answer to all of these questions is, it depends. There is no magic number or formula that dictates the size of a collection or the policies that shape it. Each community is different, and in order to serve its community, each library collection is different. What we can do is provide general recommendations by which a library can assess its collection needs and craft a collection development policy that sets its collection philosophy and guides its acquisition and retention procedures.

The first step in developing a useful policy is to analyze the collection you have. Break down the existing collection into sections that make sense with respect to your community's use. Cookbooks and travel books are good examples of sections that might be meaningful. Fiction could be broken down by genre and/or publication date.

For each section, calculate the turnover rate, an indicator that is more revealing than straight circulation. Turnover is determined by dividing the number of circulations by the number of items in that part of the collection. For example, if the section you are analyzing includes 1,000 items and that section's circulation number for the time period (usually a calendar or fiscal year) is 1,500, the turnover rate for that time period is 1.5. The higher the turnover rate, the more important that subject area or section is to your community.

Once you see what the circulation patterns are like, you can designate each section as a minimal, a moderate, or an exhaustive collection area. Once the numerical analysis is done, each section can be supplemented with anecdotal information. For example, if your library is located in a ski resort, you would probably undertake exhaustive collection of materials in the winter sports section but only minimal collection of ocean-related sports like surfing. This policy would be reinforced by a cooperative borrowing agreement with another library in an area that is more focused on summer sports. Other factors in determining the collection level include the number of patron requests for specific materials, popularity of programs in a subject area, and any local or regional initiatives or political issues of particular interest.

The policy should also include guidelines for retention periods and criteria for deselection. These sections, after approval by the trustees or other governing body, will help with your weeding plan and any resistance on the part of staff or the public when discarding materials.

Another critical factor in determining collection size, acquisition, and retention is the availability of materials within any cooperative borrowing systems your library participates in. If your patrons have easy access to regional, county, or statewide collections through materials delivery, you can be very strategic in your collection decisions. Tailor your selections to your local population's interests.

Beyond the policy that shapes your philosophy, your library must set priorities for how your space will be used. (See figure 5.1.) In the past twenty years, the activities that take place in libraries have changed and multiplied dramatically. Small-group study rooms, creation spaces, and other programs are all services that require space, and you must find that space somewhere.

FIGURE 5.1

No two libraries have the exact same stacks (and even a single library won't have the same ones over time): (*top left*) stacks in the original building, Manchester-by-the-Sea (MA) Public Library; (*top right*) stacks in the 1970s loft, Manchester-by-the-Sea (MA) Public Library; (*left*) stacks in the Dayton (OH) Metro Library.

ACCESSIBILITY

Think about your library's front door. Was the entrance built in the classical style, with the main level elevated above the street to convey monumentality and the symbolic representation of knowledge as a higher pursuit? This was a cultural norm many years ago, but it assumes that everyone entering is able-bodied.

The Americans with Disabilities Act became law in the United States nearly three decades ago, and as institutions that purport to be free to all, libraries should be 100 percent accessible. It's astonishing that many historic library buildings, revered by their communities as cultural icons, retain barriers to service and remain inaccessible well into the twenty-first century.

Types of Accessibility

Physical accessibility addresses ramps and elevators for users with impaired mobility but also for those with strollers and other equipment; all areas of the building should be accessible.

Visual accessibility includes Braille and raised-lettering signage for the visually impaired; many of these signs are required by the Americans with Disabilities Act as well as fire and building codes in all US jurisdictions.

Auditory accessibility refers to devices such as hearing loops and also emergency alarms that incorporate strobe lights in addition to auditory alarms.

Digital accessibility pertains to all digital products, primarily the library's website, which should conform to standards that allow content to be read by screen readers (including ALT (alternative text) tags for all graphic elements).

Gender accessibility is for those who do not identify as specifically female or male, which applies to restroom design.

Neurological accessibility focuses on providing spaces for those who benefit from environments with reduced visual and auditory stimulation.

FINDABILITY

This concept applies on multiple levels. First, where is the library building located? Is it in the old town center? Is it in a shopping center where people go to run errands? Is it tucked away on a side street? Is there good parking and/or a nearby public transportation stop? Are there road signs with the National Library Symbol directing drivers to the building? (See figure 5.2.) Love it or hate it, the symbol is recognizable by most Americans and has even

FIGURE 5.2
The National Library Symbol guides patrons to libraries from highways and roads across the United States.

been adopted by the Federal Highway Department. Don Norman, author of *The Design of Everyday Things*, says, "When all else fails, standardize." Using a common symbol and vocabulary, even if they're not the most beautiful or elegant, can make things much more understandable and findable.

Is the library identified on Google Maps and other commonly used online navigation tools? Are the address, hours, and contact information correct? There are few things more frustrating than going to a business during the hours Google says it's open only to find the doors locked.

What about the library's entrance? When someone finds the building, is the front door obvious when looking at the façade, or did the architect cleverly design a grand archway in a different location that's confusing from the street? Is there a sign clearly and legibly stating the name of the institution and pointing the way?

Once inside, is the layout of the building's interior intuitive? Is there a live person within sight of the entrance? Does that person look up and make eye contact with patrons as they enter? We aren't advocating a hard-sell approach whereby patrons are besieged by staff members asking if they need help at every turn. That's just annoying. Just as bad, however, is for patrons to be confronted by an unoccupied service desk or one manned by staff who have their backs turned or are looking down with concentration or, worst of all, no service point whatsoever within sight of the door.

WAYFINDING

Once inside the library, how does someone find a program, a piece of equipment, or an item in the collection? This is where wayfinding comes in. Wayfinding is a subject that planners and signage designers love, but few others understand. The word isn't even in general language dictionaries.

Wayfinding is an umbrella term that includes signage but also encompasses other visual, auditory, and tactile cues that help people navigate their way around a building or space. Things like color coding by function or floor, arrows on the wall or floor, or a recognizable device like a specific light fixture signaling a place to get help—all are examples of wayfinding—not signs exactly, but other signals that help you find your way. They are especially important for people who aren't fluent in the native language.

Wayfinding Transcends Language

An article on wayfinding by the Dutch firm /designworkplan offers these tips for crafting an effective wayfinding system:

Do not make them think
- Create a comprehensive, clear and consistent visual communication system with concise messaging.

Show only what is needed
- Show information [that is] relevant to the space, location and/or navigation path.

Remove excessive information
- Remove unnecessary elements to create a clear visual environment ahead.*

* /designworkplan, "Wayfinding," www.designworkplan.com/read/wayfinding-introduction/.

Consider the following tips for creating effective signage:

- *Don't make people think.* A sign should convey its message at a glance. Using too much text or an image that's hard to understand makes the sign useless.
- *Be clear and consistent.* Create a comprehensive visual communication system that features concise messaging and common elements. Consistency in colors, fonts, and layout helps people subconsciously recognize signs and other cues instantly.
- *Include only what is necessary.* Unnecessary words or visual elements are confusing. Design is important, but not at the expense of conveying information.
- *Present information so that navigation is intuitive.* For example, a map or directory works so much better if its orientation aligns with its location.
- *Remove excessive information and unnecessary elements.* Clarity and conciseness are essential to create a clear visual environment.

Notice a common theme here? One of the reasons some architects love wayfinding (as opposed to signage) so much is that they don't like signs cluttering up their beautiful buildings. When well designed and integrated into the space, wayfinding cues can be effective. Signs with words, however, are also needed.

A few signs are required by code, and they must be installed before the building can be occupied. These include exit signs, bathroom signs, elevator signs, and the like. In some cases, a building is opened with only the code-required signs, and the signage package is developed as the result of people's use of the space. The use of temporary signs allows for experimenting with wording and placement so that only signs that are really needed get installed. This approach can mean a better quality of sign that can be custom-designed for flexibility in light of future changes.

Some final thoughts: The signage and wayfinding system is often the last major component of a project to be funded, and many times the money has been redirected to cover shortfalls in other areas. Don't skimp. Make sure you have the funding to do it right. It will save money (and frustration) in the long run.

LIBRARY BUILDINGS

We'd love to write that the future of libraries is secure, but that would be overly optimistic. There are too many competing priorities for public funding in every city and town, and while the need for library services is clearly demonstrated, shrinking budgets, crumbling infrastructure, and inadequate facilities are common. From a facilities perspective, local funders must prioritize maintenance, ongoing improvements, and the construction of expanded or new buildings to accommodate current and future library services. (See figure 5.3.)

FIGURE 5.3

This classical façade defined the first generation of public libraries, many funded by Andrew Carnegie. To keep up with constant change and waning budgets, flexibility and openness to incremental change must define the buildings of today.

The changing library landscape is a given. When Lauren started working in a small, rural public library thirty years ago, that institution still had a paper card catalog and the only (MS-DOS) computer in the building was for bookkeeping and financial records. Today that same library has an array of technology offerings for both staff and the public, with a building that's three times the size of the original and a sophisticated computerized building management system that controls the HVAC (heating, ventilation, and air-conditioning) and other infrastructure.

Given the exponential changes in the past few decades, our imaginations fail us when we try to envision the library of thirty years in the future. The pace of developments in information technologies and consumer habits will look very different, but we can't predict how.

Buildings, even modest ones, cost millions of dollars to construct, and nobody can afford to start fresh every time a new innovation comes down the pike; neither is that a sustainable course of action. Public entities are waking up to the fact that we can't demolish and start anew as a matter of course if we want to reach the energy goals that are becoming more prevalent and necessary.

The only way to build for the future is to incorporate flexibility into all our service models and our spaces, anticipating and responding to incremental change. As Donald A. Barclay and Eric D. Scott state, in *The Library Renovation, Maintenance, and Construction Handbook,*

> The best way to accommodate the needs of the future without shortchanging the needs of the present is to plan, as much as possible, for flexibility. Conservators of rare books and manuscripts live by one golden rule: "Don't do anything to a book or manuscript that cannot be undone at a later date." While "Don't do anything to a building that cannot be undone at a later date" may be a little too extreme for building-project planners, it is not a bad goal to keep in mind.[2]

The philosophy of flexibility goes far beyond the physical building. It should serve as the foundation of the organizational culture and be a key component of the library's service design. Every decision, from policy development to how trash is handled, should be made with consideration for how to adapt and change for future needs. One of the most obstructive phrases in the library world is "That's how we've always done it."

START WHERE YOU ARE: ASSESSING YOUR SPACE

What kind of place is your library now? Your building is a physical representation of the philosophies and values held by the institution. Is this representation accurate and current? If not, why is that?

The first step in improving your space is understanding what you already have. This can be accomplished in a variety of ways, and enlisting the help of someone who isn't a regular library user for a secret shopper–style visit will provide some great information. A secret shopper is someone who comes into the library posing as a patron with the aim of evaluating the service—either something very specific or the library experience in general. The shopper makes extensive notes after the visit and reports back to the management (or whoever commissioned the visit). This is a technique used extensively in business—retail and restaurants in particular.

Let's say you want to understand how patrons navigate the library, how people find a particular item on the shelf, or why they don't understand how to print a document or sign in to your wireless system. Think of a specific goal or task (e.g., find the bathroom or locate a particular book) that a library patron may want to complete. Ask a colleague, friend, or relative who isn't familiar with the library to come in and attempt to do that thing. Ask your secret shopper to think about and document every decision point and misstep in the process. This will require the person to slow down and pay attention to the process. The shopper should also make note of any interactions with staff or other library users.

If you can't find a nonuser to do this, try it yourself with a beginner's mind-set. Pretend you don't know the building and the library's organization inside and out. Think about what it would be like to attempt the task if you were still learning the local language, for example, or if you haven't been in a library since you were in grade school. You will likely see some things that can be improved immediately, like signage or furniture placement. You might decide to move the copier to a different spot or simplify the signs. Library jargon is a particular problem; many users don't understand the difference between *circulation* and *reference* or what a proprietary database is.

Going on a service safari is fun if you approach it as the first step in a long process. (See figure 5.4.) You can divide your ideas into categories by ease of implementation or cost. Be sure to solicit the opinions of your staff (and some patrons as well, if appropriate) before you make major changes. This will create support for your process.

FIGURE 5.4
Service safaris are a good way to practice empathy and user-centered design skills and to take a first pass at identifying some small-scale usability problems you might be able to easily solve.

What You Have Now

If you've worked in a library for more than a few weeks, you already know what some of the facility-related problems are. Many building issues stem from inadequate building maintenance; outdated or poorly designed HVAC systems; leaky foundations, roofs, or windows; and the like, but those are outside our scope. In this book, we are focused on functionality and adaptability for rapid change.

Space Types

To assess your space, it's important to understand what kinds of space you have. In general, there are five basic types:

Public space includes open collections as well as seating and study areas—any areas that serve a library function and offer unrestricted public access.

Staff space refers to areas designated for staff only, such as staff workrooms, offices, and break rooms or lunchrooms.

In-between space covers areas where staff and patrons mix, like service desks, meeting rooms, enclosed study or collaboration rooms, and archives—spaces that can be used by the public but only with the knowledge of and monitoring by staff.

Storage space—there's never enough!

Unprogrammed space is an architect's term for the spaces that have to occur in any building, like hallways, stairs, restrooms, and mechanical support spaces, and are not related to library functions. These take up an average of 30 percent of the gross square footage of a library.

Clutter

One of the easiest and most productive ways to find space is decluttering. This can be difficult for librarians because we are collectors by nature and training. We love our stuff. But when we are strapped for space and want to do more, something has to give.

It's a law of nature: stuff expands to fill space. (See figure 5.5.) What's lurking in the back of your youth services storage room? Are there twenty-year-old decorations and craft supplies that someone's keeping because they might be needed someday? Sure, they might be useful at some point in the future—if anyone remembers that the stuff is there. But that real estate could be much more useful; underused closets can become spaces for tinkering, for example, or at least storage for makerspace equipment.

It's a question of priorities. Is it more important to keep a lot of stuff that might be used eventually, or will your library prioritize having a clean,

FIGURE 5.5
Clutter is the physical equivalent of baggage. It's hard to work around it and can make a service desk look uninviting. Don't think about what you need to get rid of; instead think about what you can you make room for.

fresh library with new and innovative services? This idea applies to everything. In library school, you may have learned the "just in case versus just in time" principle. This became important when digital information was fairly new and librarians were wrestling with what to keep on the shelves and what could be obtained when needed through document delivery. Paring down your physical stuff to serve your immediate needs will free up space for more and better services. Do you have a graveyard of outdated computer equipment and peripherals? Old processing supplies that are no longer used since switching to a new workflow? Broken furniture or shelving that you plan to fix when you have time? Get rid of it. Your region or state may have an electronic discussion list where you can post freebies such as these, allowing you to give useful but no longer needed stuff away to other libraries in the area or to your school library or municipal offices. If a lot of the stuff you have hanging around is just old and broken, look into disposal options. Many towns and counties have electronics recycling programs, and some electronics stores do as well.

It's just as important to reduce visual clutter—the stuff that can easily fill every surface and wall when you aren't paying attention. Lauren knows a part-time librarian who works in a tiny rural library that is housed in an old school shared with town offices. The librarian is a dedicated and thrifty person who struggles to meet the needs of residents; she has very little time and almost no money. She also has a habit of visiting the local transfer station and rescuing stuff that the library might be able to use. In one room of less than 1,000 square feet, she has crammed six sofas, several desks, and a maze of mismatched shelving. Globes, toys, and amateur artwork fill every surface and wall. When you enter the space, all you see is chaos. There is no place for the eye to rest. No doubt the librarian and the regular patrons are so used to it that the clutter has become wallpaper, fading into the background. But it's a difficult space for others, one that is unwelcoming and confusing.

Think about how your space is used. A workflow analysis can be extremely helpful in analyzing staff areas. How far, for example, does a book travel in its journey from the return drop through the sorting process before it goes back out on the floor to be shelved? What is the path of an interlibrary loan item or a new purchase from the UPS truck to the shelf?

This exercise also illustrates how intertwined space design and service design are in the user experience. Great customer service with a badly designed space is frustrating for staff as well as patrons. Likewise, a beautiful, efficient space with poor service will not result in happy patrons.

Safety and Security

Libraries should be designed with as much open space as possible. This is important for a number of reasons, including the desirability of an open and welcoming atmosphere, but its primary purpose is to allow staff to visually monitor the space without the need to physically patrol every corner of the building. Good sight lines are absolutely necessary for the safety of everyone in the library.

However, another security concern represents a conflict with this design model. It's a fact of life that we live in a world where active shooter or lockdown training has become a standard requirement for library and school staff. In such a scenario, it's highly desirable to have easily identifiable places that are out of sight of the assailant and self-contained, lockable rooms. How is it possible to reconcile these needs?

There are no easy answers. Planning ahead, having written policies and procedures, and, most important, conducting regular staff training, is essential. Seek the help of your local experts and involve them in the development of the plan and should identify escape routes and potential hiding places. Have them review the final plan and conduct staff training sessions. The Department of Homeland Security offers some resources that can help you start planning.[3]

A new safety need has arisen as we anticipate reopening libraries in the aftermath of the COVID-19 pandemic. The need to accommodate social distancing will require creativity in the rearrangement of library spaces and operational procedures for the short term. This will likely have long-term impacts on the way we design libraries, the furniture and equipment we purchase, and the service models we adopt.

Service Points

Does your main public service desk present immediate barriers? Is it large and monumental, separating staff from patrons visually or physically? Does the sign include library jargon? Words like *circulation* and *reference* are opaque to the general public, and a sign reading "Circulation Desk" or "Reference Desk" can be confusing to those unfamiliar with those terms. Many libraries are using "Checkout" or "Information" as replacements.

The trend in service points is to create smaller kiosk-type stations that allow staff to interact with the public more directly through a design that permits staff to easily exit their stations to accompany patrons to their desired service areas. If this isn't practical, especially in small libraries with minimal staff, a desk with a larger surface area is fine, but it should still be configured so that staff can easily come out from behind it. A desk with a variable-height surface (electric, hydraulic, or hand crank) is an excellent option because it allows the desk to be set at the optimal height for patrons (e.g., small children and those using a wheelchair) and provides better ergonomics for staff.

Many libraries are also adopting a policy that directs staff members to be attentive to the public at all times when on desk duty, rather than bringing projects and other tasks to work on when they aren't busy. This service model promotes the idea that when staff are on the desk, that's their sole responsibility for that time span and they should be helping patrons, roaming, or otherwise paying attention to that task. If they are roaming or must leave the desk to help a patron in another part of the building, they should carry a cell phone, a pager, or another alerting device so that they can be summoned back to the service desk when it gets busy. If this service model is adapted, it's important to implement shorter rotating shifts on the desk as well as scheduled time off-desk for staff to complete other tasks. Being on-desk for more than two or three hours at a time is exhausting.

Self-Service

Another rapidly evolving trend in libraries is the move to self-service options for patrons. With self-checkout appearing in many grocery and drugstores, and with the juggernaut of Amazon transforming every aspect of retail in the United States, quick, efficient self-service should be available for those who want it. Note that we are not advocating for the replacement of staffed desks, as there will always be users who prefer face-to-face interactions and problems that can't be solved through self-service options.

Self-Checkout

Besides copy and printing services, self-checkout is the most common and pervasive self-service option in libraries so far. Self-check equipment is available from numerous vendors and can be implemented through virtually all ILS software packages. The goal is to improve the experience for those who, for example, like to place items on hold from the ILS and then quickly stop in to retrieve and check out the items themselves. This not only provides a streamlined process but also reduces congestion at the service desk and frees up staff to focus on more substantive tasks, improving job satisfaction and reducing repetitive motion injuries.

Self-Service Holds Pickup

The corollary to self-checkout is open hold pickup. For patrons like those described in the previous section, the efficiency of their transactions is derailed if they have to wait in line at the desk to obtain the items on hold from a staff member. For library staff and patrons who are concerned about patron privacy, it's easy to anonymize titles by shelving hold items spine-in, with a paper label that includes the patron's last name along with the date that the hold expires. Individual patrons can also elect to have their holds held behind a staff service point upon request.

Taking this a step further, after-hours hold pickup lockers add even more convenience for people who are unable to visit the library during regular business hours. These can be embedded in the exterior wall (allowing staff to fill them from inside) or be free-standing units placed in a night lobby or outside the building, similar to Amazon lockers outside 7-Eleven stores. Materials are checked out to patrons prior to being placed in the locker.

Laptop Vending Machines

As libraries move away from fixed desktop workstations and toward mobile devices for in-library use, laptop/tablet vending machines are a secure way for users to borrow this equipment. The machine is operated by scanning a valid library card and releasing the chosen mobile device to the patron. The loan period is customizable, and the device is locked and unusable after the loan period expires. The patron must return it to the correct slot in the machine. Laptop lockers are also operated in a similar way, but the device must be plugged into the charger cord as an additional step. A less expensive but accordingly less self-service-friendly alternative to laptop vending machines are laptop carts unlockable by staff. They have some good selling points too: they don't take up much space, they feature great cable management (i.e., they require only one cord plugged into the wall), and their mobility allows for easy deployment at programs and classes.

Express Service Points

Libraries can extend their outreach via electronic express service points. Book and audiovisual media vending machines are effective in busy locations like train stations and airports, as well as grocery stores. Some libraries are even implementing staffless library services using products like Bibliotheca's open+. These spaces, often a small enclosed area that's part of a larger library building, can be accessed by patrons who have received special training. These areas contain small, high-interest collections and hold pickup with self-check-out as well as public access computers. They sometimes also provide a hotline to access live help from a staffed desk at a remote location.

Self-service is nothing new. Years ago, library collections were closed and only librarians could enter the sacred stacks. Every library has a self-service book return slot. Copy and microform machines are operated by patrons without staff intervention (well, mostly). Some patrons (and staff) may have fears about the potential for lost jobs due to the growth of self-service options, but these concerns can be laid to rest with the explanation that the goal is not to reduce staff. It's to provide more and better services while keeping operational costs down. It's truly a benefit to everyone, and it's there for those who want it.

ANTICIPATING FUTURE SPACE NEEDS

A fundamental conflict exists between the concept of bricks-and-mortar buildings and constant change. Buildings are expensive, and it's not possible to rebuild every time a new service is implemented. It's wasteful both financially and in terms of environmental sustainability.

Yesterday the trend was makerspaces. Today it's the Library of Things. What's next? Nobody knows, and buildings last at least fifty years. It's futile to try to anticipate what's coming down the road, so planning for maximum flexibility is crucial.

The recent library shutdown and social distancing measures required as the result of the COVID-19 pandemic argue strongly in favor of planning for flexibility. It's very difficult to adapt rigid, built-in shelving and furniture to allow for greater space between people, whereas mobile items can be reconfigured to accommodate new and quickly changing requirements.

From an architectural standpoint, this means that all interior walls should be removable partitions rather than load-bearing walls. Elements that are difficult or impossible to move, like bathrooms and elevators, are ideally located along the perimeter of the building. This ensures that when interior reconfigurations are required, the structure and other systems are not compromised.

Flexibility in Library Design

Flexibility should be a guiding principle in planning a new or renovated/expanded library, but it's also possible to incorporate small, incremental changes in existing spaces and to inject more flexibility. According to the Project for Public Spaces, "The complexity of public spaces is such that you cannot expect to do everything right initially. The best spaces experiment with short term improvements that can be tested and refined over many years!"[4]

Plan for the Long Haul

These are some of the basic principles of flexible design:

- Design for as many open spaces with non-load-bearing partition walls as possible.
- Place elements such as bathrooms, elevators, and stairs along the perimeter of the building.
- Use furniture instead of millwork for service points and cabinetry.
- Incorporate as much mobile furniture, shelving, and equipment as possible.

We have to let go of the phrase "That's how we've always done it" because that *always* time frame is getting shorter and shorter. Flexibility applies to thinking and working, not just spaces and technology.

Try to view every decision with end users in mind. How will it affect them? How will it affect staff? For example, let's say that you want to implement a new collection of widgets for public use. From the staff's point of view, consider these questions:

- What kind of storage will the widgets require?
- Are the widgets particularly expensive and need extra security?
- How will this new collection affect workflow for staff?
- Will extra staff time be needed for handling and/or helping people use the widgets?
- Will staff require training to provide support?
- What kind of special containers or tagging will the processors need to use for this new collection?

Then think about the situation from a patron's point of view: imagine that you are a user borrowing the item, or ask a regular user to be a test subject.

- Will the widgets be for in-library use or will users take them home?
- What is the loan period? Will overdue fines apply, and if so, how much?
- Will extra training be needed to use the widgets?
- Are adequate instructions included or available?
- Are training sessions available?

Use the same mind-set for every change in service or space you are contemplating. Ask frontline staff to role-play as patrons and act out the service change scenario. For alterations to spaces, create mock-ups of walls, furniture, and equipment using low-cost materials like cardboard boxes and tape on the floor.

If you want to provide a new service, think about the space required, not only for the service itself but for any storage and staff-related spaces as well. If you don't already have extra space to accommodate the new activity or collection, here are three ways to gain space:

- Add physical space by building an addition or constructing an entirely new building.
- Reconfigure existing space through conversion of underused or poorly configured existing areas or elimination or reduction of an existing service or collection.
- Create a multiuse space by adding flexible furnishings and equipment to an existing space so that it can serve more than one function.

The Everything Store: A Case Study in Flexibility

The library at Olin College of Engineering is an example of a space trying to be all things to all people. Olin is tiny, boasting a total campus population (including staff, faculty with various statuses, and students) of around 600. Aside from the dorms, where all students live for the duration of their studies, Olin has just three buildings, including the one in which the library takes up about 8,000 square feet. The library is open to Oliners via 24/7 keycard access, which works out surprisingly well; the worst things ever found by the staff are forgotten dining hall dishes and questionably large pieces of cardboard. It's also one of just a handful of spaces on campus suited to hosting events, whether workshops, talks, weekend gatherings for alumni and parents, or welcome-back breakfasts. The library staff are constantly moving furniture around to accommodate these different uses and also observing how people are using the space when something special isn't going on and they're just looking for somewhere to hang out or study.

The library also circulates camera and audio recording equipment, charging and display cables, and hand tools. It has its own sewing machines, vinyl cutters, a screen printer, and a podcasting studio; it also hosts a clutch of 3-D printers, run by experts from the campus machine shop. In addition to all of that, it has print volumes and periodicals, a small archive, a quiet reading room, and four rooms for group or individual study. It's a careful balancing act to provide enough space, for both active use and storage, for all of these wide-ranging activities in just 8,000 square feet; staff are always trying to rethink, reposition, or relabel things. There's no silver bullet solution for how to accommodate all of this, and staff are committed to always considering new ideas as they're suggested (that's not to say they're all implemented, but they *are* considered!). However, from her experience at Olin, Callan does have some thoughts on how to scaffold flexibility in spaces and what sorts of furniture and equipment can help you get the job done.

- *Get shelves on casters for high-traffic areas where you might like to hold events or make extra space on demand.* Don't cheap out on this. It's tempting to skimp on things like wheels or to use do-it-yourself solutions; but books are heavy, bookshelves are very heavy, and bookshelves full of books are very, very heavy. You want heavy-duty swiveling wheels that will help, not hinder, you when you start pushing these things around. (See figure 5.6.) Consider getting shelves that are relatively short; these will give you the added bonus of better sight lines whether they're in their usual place or they're pushed off to one side or another.

FIGURE 5.6
Mobile shelving can be pricey, but it's highly recommended if you are strapped for space and are looking for ways to reinvent and repurpose areas to accommodate different types of use throughout the day. This shelving by Opto is in the Whistler (BC) Public Library.

- *Pay attention to how people are using spaces most of the time.* In response to what you actually observe, give them options for engaging with spaces differently and make thoughtful delineations. For instance, at Olin, staff observed two main modes of interacting in the spaces on the open-plan first floor.

The first was a lounge mode on the couches or comfy armchairs more conducive to socializing, club chats, or casual meetings; the second was a study mode characterized by sitting and working at tables alone or in groups. When Callan started at Olin, the lounge furniture and study furniture were commingled throughout the library, but now the floor is separated into two areas defined by the furniture based on users' behavior patterns. This makes it easier for staff to accommodate these two types of uses simultaneously and for students to choose one side or the other. This use separation also had the unintended but happy consequence of making it easier to reconfigure the space as a whole: the heavier study tables are pushed flush against the same wall on the study side instead of positioned across the library from one another, which makes it much easier to alter the lounge side to accommodate larger events.

- *Choose wheels over walls.* Don't just mount whiteboards to one side of the room or the other; get wheeled versions that can move around with the other furniture. The library at Olin has an Idea Harvester, a thirty-two-inch flat-screen TV mounted to repurposed library shelves on wheels; it also has a large roll of paper that staff can pull down over the opposite side for taking notes and sketching. Under consideration at the time of this writing is getting a food and drink cart to help staff easily move a discussion, meeting, or small party from one place to another. This would be an accommodation for the long counter at the front of the library, which is great for queueing up and self-serving food but lousy for sitting down and eating it. People often want to graze but don't want to move back and forth between the counter and the more comfortable seating areas. Using a cart would give staff the option to reposition events as we need to without a lot of mess or running back and forth.
- *If you're getting powered furniture, make sure you have somewhere to plug it in.* This sounds obvious, but it's something not everyone has put into practice. You can buy furniture with modular power distribution too; some tables allow you to plug in on one side or the other or move the cabling around entirely, so you don't need to be concerned about whether or not you can move the furniture to plug it in.
- *Speaking of power, think about how to distribute it more creatively and with modular options.* A few different services offer under-the-carpet or trench wiring solutions that lay flat on the ground but don't require any permanent alterations to a building. These approaches can be especially useful if the construction or foundations of a building make it impossible to core the floors

but the walls are very far apart. Also, if you've got the money and competent contractors to do the work, going outside the building is a possibility too. At the Public Library of Brookline in Massachusetts, Callan worked on a project to move staff computers to an unused mezzanine area that needed to be able to support fourteen data drops and at least as many power outlets. The wiring was too unsightly to run it through the library, so she chose to have the electricians route it outside into a covered utility box in order for it to discreetly reach the mezzanine floor.

- *When you're selecting furniture, think of all of the different ways people might want to sit as they study, hang out, or read.* Patrons' use of furniture can vary from day to day or task to task. They might want couches or benches for more casual reading or hangout time; they might want tables or desks and chairs for more focused study time. There's plenty of variation among each type of furniture. Take the Boston Public Library's central branch, renovated in 2016, where there's at least two dozen kinds of seating on offer. They have small tables and large tables. They have high-top counters that flank the sides of the building. They have study tables with one, two, or four chairs in low-, medium-, or high-traffic areas. They have couches, café tables, and benches. On a much smaller scale, Olin's neighbors at Babson College have a greenhouse that is meant to look like an indoor park. It features high ceilings, lots of glass to let the light in, live trees, and park benches and picnic tables mixed in with sofas, high-top counters, and more conventional chairs. This is a beautiful way to help students weather the long, gray New England winters. You don't need a huge amount of space to justify investing in a healthy variety of seating options; just get inspired by the options at other libraries and think about what might work for your own patrons.

As libraries of all kinds increasingly embrace flexibility, be on the lookout for inspiration whenever you visit other campuses or communities. Ideas can also be adapted from spaces other than libraries, like retail stores, parks, hotels, or airports. Observing and asking your own patrons is the best way to know what they need or would like to have; based on their own travels and experiences in other kinds of places, they might have innovative solutions for the space challenges you've been trying to figure out.

NOTES

1. Ranganathan. S. R., *The Five Laws of Library Science* (Madras: Madras Library Association, 1931), https://catalog.hathitrust.org/Record/001661182.
2. Donald A. Barclay and Eric D. Scott, *The Library Renovation, Maintenance, and Construction Handbook* (Chicago: Neal-Shuman, 2011), 11.
3. Cybersecurity and Infrastructure Security Agency, "Active Shooter Preparedness," US Department of Homeland Security, last revised September 11, 2019, www.dhs.gov/active-shooter.
4. Project for Public Spaces, "Eleven Principles for Creating Great Community Places," www.pps.org/article/11steps.

PART III
Fortitude

In this section, we offer boots-on-the-ground ideas for responding to the needs identified so far. We address making small changes as a part of larger-scale efforts and trying new ideas to continue gathering feedback along the way. Last, we discuss threats to the profession and how we can strengthen our defenses for confronting them together.

6
Project Management and Problem Solving

Whether you are a frontline worker or an administrator, you will be called upon at some point to manage a project of some description, whether it's collating a set of handouts or overseeing the construction of a new building. Any project of any size can be approached with UX principles foremost in your mind.

SMALL PROBLEMS

If you're just getting started with a new job and you're feeling overwhelmed by everything that needs to be done, it can be irritating to hear about the small stuff, problems that seem inconsequential or something that should have been taken care of long ago. Imagine circulating a survey in which you're asking for big ideas and you hear from people who want you to stock more paper clips. Are they just missing the point? Do they not care about your visions of an ultramodern, user-obsessed, world-class library? In all likelihood, the answer to both is probably not. If people answer "If you had infinite resources, what would you change about the library?" with "Get more staples and tape," there's a good chance no one has asked for their input for a long time. There's also no sense in getting frustrated by this. It gives you a hugely easy win—just order the damn paper clips. The one part of this that's a little trickier than meets the eye is recognizing when the process of satisfying the small suggestions needs some more structure to it. If people really are wondering why it's impossible to find staples or printer paper, you probably need to keep a simple inventory and schedule supply orders.

Solving small problems can uncover slightly larger problems. To keep on this theme of office supplies, if you can't keep enough of them on hand, is it maybe because you don't have anywhere to put them? This might sound ridiculous, but Callan does work in a library where there is no storage closet. Though the lack of a closet is something everyone is well aware of, it's not a solution the community is going to pitch to the library, nor is it the sort of thing the library can expect a successful alumnus to want to fund. It's a great example of a medium-sized problem.

MEDIUM PROBLEMS

Medium-sized problems are the kinds of things you don't necessarily hear from patrons who are responding to surveys, but that your staff could probably rattle off without thinking twice. They're unsexy but annoying enough to slow down workflow or lead to dissatisfaction that might be tough for your users to readily identify. They often have a lot to do with building features or layout, such as lighting, furniture, or lack of space. You might be able to chip away at these things by repurposing money in your budget or using unrestricted funds, or you might need to rip things out entirely and rethink them. Either way, you and your staff are likely on your own for this kind of thing. (See figure 6.1.)

FIGURE 6.1
Every crisis leaves us at a fork in the road. Will we continue down the path we already know or try to find our way along a new one that presents itself?

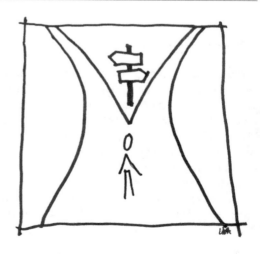

In the case of the missing closet, we took a critical look at the various ersatz storage solutions that had formed under desks and other surfaces and the kinds of things that had accumulated in them. We had two four-by-four-foot storage units full of napkins, plastic silverware, and paper plates but nary a box of tissues or replacement staples. Why? We were suffering the usual clutter trap of libraries: we were holding on to junk that we thought we'd need someday, worrying that we wouldn't find the money for it later.

We're not saying you should throw things out for the sake of it (we wound up giving most of our unneeded stuff to student groups and other departments). Just don't hoard things when you're fretting about space simply because you went to a conference where half the program titles followed the format of the aforementioned "How to Do [Insert Important Library Task] on a Shoestring Budget." In fact, let's dump *shoestring budget* entirely, at least as a motivational phrase. The whole "Do more with less" mentality is unhealthy and burnout inducing, not scrappy and creative. Doing more with less is not something to be celebrated; it's something to overcome, to be fought back and advocated against. Although we librarians hate wasting things and want to see our libraries aspiring to much greater levels of sustainability, we can't cling to our boxes of disintegrating rubber bands and expect a budget increase. We need to show off and fight for all we do and be thoughtful stewards of our spaces in the meantime.

BIG PROBLEMS

What's a big problem in the library world? Well, there's the kind you can plan for and the kind that comes out of nowhere. The out-of-nowhere kind tends to take the form of facilities issues, natural disasters, or random tragedies. Simply put, responding to a crisis is the hardest thing you'll ever have to do at work, and no amount of preparation will lead to you handling it without a hitch. The COVID-19 pandemic that we're living through during this writing is a big problem not only for libraries but for just about every aspect of human life on earth. Libraries all over the world are prototyping like mad, trying and failing and trying again, and even in the midst of chaos, this is exciting to see. The long-term impact on how we live and work won't be known for a long time, and we're all doing the best we can in the face of extreme uncertainty.

Other big problems are more localized. Callan lost a coworker in a fatal bike accident about a mile away from the branch where they worked. This person was a beloved member of the community, a fixture in the lives of countless children and families. The news broke in *The Boston Globe* before anyone in administration had heard. The library reached out for help from the police department and the town administrator's office, both of which have more experience in handling a tragedy. With their assistance, library leadership crafted a public statement and brought a grief counselor to the branch. Meanwhile, they had to tell the staff what was going on. Some of them had already heard; the branch staff was tightly knit. Everyone was shocked and devastated, no matter how close or distant they were to their fallen colleague. The library scheduled both private and public memorials to give staff the chance to share their memories and thoughts with one another; they weren't asked to come to the public memorial unless they thought it would help. When something like this happens, it's essential to provide backup for people on the front lines and emotional support for the whole staff for as long as they need it—and don't hesitate to get advice and support from other departments.

As for the other type of big problem, the kind you see coming or maybe are irritated by every day, you may or may not be able to solve it in the short term. You should try, of course, but large-scale projects in libraries often move at a snail's pace, especially if they're infrastructural at all. A building renovation, furniture replacement, or network equipment upgrade are all examples of this. These things require capital improvements or budget expansions, which (for the most part, anyway) don't tend to get approved overnight. So what can you do to make a dent on these bigger issues in the meantime?

One of the first things we suggest is that you need to wrap your head around your budget completely, whether you're responsible for just a small chunk of it or you're running the whole show. This is much easier said than done, but it's worth the effort. Municipal and academic accounting software leaves a lot to be desired, in our experience; plus, it doesn't help that every system and institution handles such things differently. Still, there's a general pattern of codes and line items that mostly everyone follows. One trick we recommend is digging deep into prior years' expenditures to try to find two things: (1) stuff that was unnecessarily or mistakenly paid for (yes, both of these things happen) and (2) costs that you almost certainly won't incur again (e.g., for one-time consultations or software you're discontinuing). We suspect you might find more money to spend in your current fiscal cycle than you think you have. If you have more money than you expected, you might be able to chip off chunks of bigger projects here and there, like buying new chairs and tables for a small section of the building versus the whole top-to-bottom thing.

You should also try to identify projects that really are just up to the library, in terms of how money is spent or which stakeholders are impacted. If you have trust funds or other types of gifts, find out the rules governing how to spend those funds. (Side note: if you ever have an opportunity to take in new gift funds, ask your donors to make their gifts as unrestricted as possible.) Focusing on projects that are the purview of the library and don't require other people's input or signoff is also a good place to start. For instance, when Callan started her job at Olin College, there were two roads to go down to address the many issues impacting patrons' access to information: one was to replace the challenging ILS that required constant triage from staff; the other was to jump headlong into a conversation with faculty about academic database subscriptions.

Callan and her staff opted for the former for two reasons: (1) the ILS is the foundational technology of any library and they at least needed to have that part of their house in order, and (2) working on this didn't require that they schedule meetings or try to capture interest or bandwidth that was lacking from faculty members. This isn't to diminish the importance of the conversation about scholarly publishing and the serials crisis; it's just to say that as a staff of three, they had to rank the urgency and feasibility or each option so they could choose one over the other. Identifying a big problem and then *not* leaping in and attempting to solve it immediately is a tough thing to do, but you have to be able to prioritize. You also have to be able to find opportunities where you can make progress, even if some or all of the larger-scale stuff has to wait. This is where a good strategic plan can really come in handy. It can help you connect your efforts in a way that will enable you and your stakeholders to see that you *are* trying to answer their concerns and you *are* getting things done, even if they're not *the* thing.

Another big problem we've encountered is what we call the ad hoc library, which is the kind where nothing is documented, information is trapped in the brains of a select few and available nowhere else, and processes and workflows are being followed out of adherence to past practice but no other definable reason. It's the kind of workplace that's about to collapse in on itself at any time, which has a negative and perceptible impact on the folks working there—they run around in a constant state of present shock, trying to keep the trains running on a given day but forgetting about the rest of the weekly schedule. This situation can develop because of weak or inept management, low staffing, or a history of people who didn't really know what they were doing learning from other people who didn't really know what they were doing (no judgment—we've all been there).

Luckily enough, it's not hard to course-correct these situations. Often this requires just a second set of eyes—any set, not even one that necessarily has previous management experience in the brain behind it—to reevaluate what's going on. Just as bad signage or dirty carpets can fade into the background for people who've been working at the same place for years, so, too, can the difficulty or clunkiness of a given workflow. Staffing or other changes can throw off existing systems too. One person benefits from an e-mail alias to manage interlibrary loan requests; ten people benefit from a ticketing system wherein they can all see who has claimed or responded to a request, review the conversation history, and jump in to help if needed. If you're the person responsible for this clunkiness, you'll find your professional contacts are an invaluable resource for gut-checking yourself and helping you consider alternatives. You aren't going it alone; thousands of people are doing something *pretty* close to your job, and dozens if not hundreds are doing something *very* close to it. Use that collective wisdom to your advantage as you work on settling down the rat race—no reinvented wheels!

PROBLEMS OF ANY SIZE

There's a lot to be said for project management tools. Despite their corporate origin, you don't have to pay through the nose for these; they're often free up to a certain level and inexpensive past that. They work well in tandem with tools for communicating and sharing that go beyond the e-mail inbox. There are so many of these technologies out there—Slack, Asana, Google Drive, Microsoft Teams, Miro, and Trello, just to rattle off several—that you can pick and choose different ones for different purposes and knit them into one big interoperable pile of more efficient workflows than shared e-mail addresses and folders can get you.

Project management tools can get conversations and ideas flowing. They can map out small, medium, and large problems and not only help delegate action items that will work toward solving them but also give you a sense of positive momentum toward getting things done—and a record of everything you've accomplished. In Libraryland where our goals and plans are mostly self-generated, it's important to remember to share those goals and plans with as many people as possible and to celebrate accomplishments as they're made. Having a record makes sharing this information easier and also helps tremendously if you have to write any kind of self-evaluation of your work or an annual report. It's much easier to find that information in a digital list of what you've been working on than it is to hunt and peck through related messages in your e-mail.

If you have a strategic plan and you're looking to get started with a project management tool, pop the plan right in there. Most of these tools use some system of boards versus lists versus tasks; for instance, event planning is a board, FY22 programming plans is a list, and selecting panelists for a talk is a task. You can separate your strategic planning themes or principles into boards. If you've got an action plan—a typically year-long set of steps to help you meet your strategic goals—to match up with those principles, you can start creating and assigning tasks that way. For example, let's say you have the theme "Welcoming the Community" and the related action plan item "Translating endcap signs into multiple languages." "Welcoming the Community" is the board, "Translating endcap signs into multiple languages" becomes a list, and then you can create related tasks, such as "Identify language proficiencies among staff members" and "Redesign the sign templates to be more readable and user-friendly."

Many of these tools then give you the ability to assign tasks to specific people on your team; you (or they) can also set deadlines. This way, people know what is expected of them and when. The collaborative nature of these tools also gives people a chance to participate in the definition of a goal or the steps to take to achieve it. They won't just be complying with orders passed down from on high; they'll be participating in the definition and execution of those orders in a way that gives them more agency and buy-in.

DOCUMENTATION: AVOIDING LEARNING CLIFFS

When Callan started her job at the Public Library of Brookline, there wasn't much to help her figure things out. A few drawerfuls of old notebooks, yellowing personnel memos, and mysterious keys were left behind in the office she inherited. Because of the exact sort of siloing around technology jobs discussed in chapter 4, none of the staff members had been cross-trained on much of anything that was now her responsibility. A colleague remarked, "Bit of a learning curve, huh?" Callan said, "Well, it's really been more of a learning *cliff*"—not a gradient upward, but a freefall into the knowledge gaps.

Face it: you're not going to be at your job forever. Libraries work on a different timescale than you do; they are cultural institutions that we expect will endure, and while we don't know what the future holds for technology writ large, your choices today will impact their use and sustainability going forward. The best thing you can do to sustain technology in the library is to document what you're doing as you do it, or as soon after as you can, and save your documentation in multiple formats and places.

Set up a folder on your desktop called HOW TO DO EVERYTHING or something similarly all-encompassing. Use a password manager like LastPass, which offers a service for teams that are looking to easily share log-in credentials or people who are just trying to keep track of their own. In your master documentation folder, make subfolders that represent categories of knowledge you can be pretty sure will be useful beyond your tenure: lists of vendors and invoices, budget information, special setups or basic tutorials for software or hardware that doesn't have many guides available on the open web, equipment inventories, and anything else that might get left in your brain when your brain leaves. If there is a particularly helpful quick start guide or manual for a piece of technology that you use often, save it and file it away in a place that makes sense.

Consider making a publicly viewable version of this documentation as well as your own local version and make it accessible to as many people as you can. Technologists tend to hoard knowledge, but this won't suit them in the library setting because it creates unnecessary bottlenecks by limiting the work that can be delegated. If you're not comfortable with this approach, products such as Springshare's LibAnswers, mentioned in chapter 4, can help you create a knowledge base generated from questions that truly are frequently asked. You can limit to whom you grant access to this information either way; just think about the rationale for the limitation. Is it because you think people will break something (or because they think they'll break it)? Is it because they aren't tech people? Think about how you can mitigate the effects of anything they might break and give some thought to why certain tasks are left to only technologists versus other staff. We suspect you could delegate a lot more than you are.

We advocate for doing this work as you go along, but if you know you will be leaving your job, be sure to leave something behind for the person taking over. It'd be great if this went without saying, but in our experience, that's not how it works. Documentation of everything we've already mentioned is most important, but you might also have some especially valuable thoughts on what might need some attention a few years down the road. It can be really liberating to jot down these issues with the knowledge that you won't have to deal with them. For instance, let's say you know your public computer monitors are on their last legs but you just couldn't find the money to pay for new ones with everything else you had going on in a given year. Let your successor know that the problem exists so that person won't be caught unawares when the stands start to fall apart or the power buttons get stuck. This is a win-win; you won't have to deal with it and the person coming in after you won't be taken by surprise. We recommend writing out a bunch of immediate priorities for the next person to think about and take on after assuming your position, giving that person a road map for what to focus on and some context about your own decision making.

7
Horizon Scanning for Threats

Looking at the future of libraries can be scary. We are threatened from all sides by those who see us as irrelevant, unnecessary, or not worth the cost. The COVID-19 pandemic made these threats clearer than ever as library staff around the United States were forced to continue going to work despite the dangers or were laid off or furloughed in counties and cities throughout the country because administrators said they couldn't "allow employees to work at home and get paid with taxpayer dollars if they have no work to do."[1] Even as municipalities and higher education institutions permitted staff to stay at home with pay, stressful conversations about budgets are haunting library workers around the country. Our values of privacy and freedom are under attack by profiteers and surveillance capitalism. How can we maintain and strengthen our position?

PERCEIVED IRRELEVANCE

The recent COVID-19 pandemic forced the temporary closure of public libraries around the world. Our final draft took shape in our homes, as we were sheltering in place. As we've mentioned, the long-term impacts of this global event are unknown at the time of this writing, but many jurisdictions have already been tempted to reduce library staffing and resources in the face of a tanked economy. The closures have also brought back the perennial question, "Why do we need libraries at all when everything's online?" It's clear that libraries, along with other institutions, need a strong plan for anticipating similar future events.

There was plenty for library workers to get angry about during the spring of 2020 as they struggled to be included in states' emergency and reopening plans, but adding insult to injury was an April report from the Johns Hopkins Center for Health Security. This document outlined approaches for safe reopening for various kinds of businesses and organizations, and it identified public libraries as "low risk" for transmission.[2] It was swiftly shot down by library workers,[3] who know that on a routine workday, they see hundreds of people, handle materials, touch surfaces, share computers, assist with technology use, clean all manner of messes, and conduct checkout and reference transactions, all typically from much less than six feet away. This has been the norm for some time now, so how did the researchers not have a clue? What image of a library did they have in their heads?

We need better representation of our current image, and we need to find a broad coalition of support for our efforts, not only right now but to keep us afloat in the future. The Electronic Frontier Foundation and its work around removing barriers to broadband access, various subsets of the ACLU and its work around digital privacy rights, community groups fighting for racial justice, and alliances of teachers, social workers, advocates for decarceration and police abolition, and countless others come to mind.

We need to fight the ideas that we're irrelevant, that everything we do is online, and that our buildings are just a bunch of empty peaceful reading rooms. While the pandemic provided an opportunity for libraries to promote and augment their digital services and resources, to reduce our work to just that dismisses the needs of our most vulnerable patrons who have no internet access or even shelter of any kind. Library workers know that patrons will want to get back to their normal routines of visiting the physical library, especially if they live alone, have children, or are people with disabilities. We know that libraries serve a role as a special place where residents feel safe and secure, where they're part of the community and are able to ask for help. For the sake of the people who need us most, we must push back against this commodification and oversimplification of what we do.

CENSORSHIP BY A THOUSAND INVOICES

In fall 2019, back in those more innocent days before the pandemic, officials in Citrus County, Florida, denied a local library's request for funding its subscription to the *New York Times*.[4] The county commissioners laughed at the thought of paying for the paper, especially for digital access to it; one asked, "Why the heck would we spend money on something like that?" Another commissioner called the paper "fake news," saying "I agree with President Trump. . . . I will not be voting for this. I don't want the New York Times in this county." Should an official's political views be grounds for deciding what content a library can make available? How about a publisher's profit margins?

At the beginning of November 2019, Macmillan, one of the five largest publishers in the United States, declared they would begin instating embargoes on all libraries looking to obtain multiple copies of new e-books until eight weeks after their release date in order to boost paper book sales.[5] Although there is no proof that libraries have a negative impact on book sales, digital or otherwise, the embargo is a decision that undermines the work librarians have done to democratize access to information in the past century and a half.

According to the American Library Association, Macmillan's restriction limits libraries' ability to provide access to information for all. It particularly harms library patrons with disabilities or learning issues: "EBooks become large-print books with a few clicks, and most eBook readers offer fonts and line spacing that make reading easier for people with dyslexia."[6] As one librarian wrote in an editorial for Publisher's Weekly,

> While Macmillan's e-book embargo aims to squeeze a few more sales out of frustrated library users, it unfairly disadvantages e-book readers who use the library out of need. Equal access to information regardless of ability to pay is foundational to a democratic society and is why public libraries exist.[7]

It may not be as blatantly censorious as what the Citrus County commissioners are up to, but the embargo prevents people from being able to read what they want to read when and how they want to read it.

Macmillan did lift the embargo during the COVID-19 crisis,[8] but who knows for how long? No matter what the publisher chooses to do next, Macmillan's e-book policy presents a problem for libraries that amounts to censorship by a thousand invoices. By pricing out libraries or denying them access altogether, companies are limiting what people can read and, in the process, creating a user experience so frustrating that many people give up on it. Streaming media platforms are another challenge. There is not much conversation happening about how libraries can provide institutional access to services like Netflix, Hulu, or Amazon Prime. When librarians try to engage in agreements with these companies, they tend to hear nothing back. We're so far out of their line of sight because we aren't profitable. After all, our business model is essentially "Take very small amounts of money from people through taxes or tuition and translate it back into lots of free stuff for those same people to use." Theirs is "Charge lots of people quite a bit of money for just enough access to things they like that they keep autopaying their subscriptions." The two don't mesh well.

This situation is bad because at some point in the near future, the physical media libraries can easily provide access to in the form of DVDs will cease to be a viable option for many borrowers. In early 2019, Samsung announced it was going to stop manufacturing Blu-ray players.[9] Libraries are already contending with certain shows and movies available exclusively through streaming services and never being sold as physical copies. This is only the beginning as we move into an era where DVDs become a thing of the past and theatrical releases go straight to streaming, again creating a division of access based on who has or doesn't have the $9.99/month for a Netflix account (and the $9.99/month for a Hulu account, and the $6.99/month for a Disney+ account, and the cable subscription for an HBO GO account, etc.).

Libraries will have to think about how to contend with this shift to subscription models and pricey digital copies for just about everything as content becomes increasingly disembodied from its discrete physical form. If Macmillan doesn't back down and other big publishers join in, will libraries boycott or keep patrons chugging along through the slow holds queue? Is there a way forward through developing institutional memberships for the biggest streaming media services? If so, would they be prohibitively expensive? What about the patron privacy implications? Tech companies are fond of subsidizing lower costs by selling behavioral data. If libraries can't afford these services or can't offer them ethically, they might need to consider other options. Can libraries get by with just stocking the shelves with foreign, specialized, or forgotten titles that don't find their way into streaming format? We don't have the answers, but librarians need to be talking about this canary in the coal mine.

OTHER DUTIES AS ASSIGNED

COVID-19 shone a light on the degree to which the social safety net has collapsed in the United States, and how library workers are often burdened with the fallout. The initial resistance to public libraries closing to the public in many urban areas seemed to be an open confession that cities don't have the infrastructure or mechanisms to step in and assist folks in need of shelter and child care and instead expect library staff to continue bearing that burden as they normally do. As of this writing, some areas have gone so far as to lay off library workers and ask them to instead staff emergency shelters with minimal training and protection.[10] While working on advocacy efforts for libraries during the pandemic, Callan discovered from talking to library workers that this had been going on in other forms for much longer in disaster-prone areas like Houston, Texas, and Palm Beach County, Florida. This is an ideological threat to libraries coming from austerity-minded public officials that we should prepare to combat much more of in the belt-tightening years sure to come as the country begins its recovery.

As we write, the biggest threats to library staff all over the country are that (1) local jurisdictions are forcing their employees to take on dangerous duties so they don't lose their paychecks and (2) employees are being laid off and furloughed in unprecedented numbers. To protect against abuses of power, library workers need to find meaningful resources and alliances for advocacy and self-preservation. Labor laws and union power vary widely from state to state, as do the key stakeholders in any given municipality or at the state level. We have professional organizations that champion library-as-institution, but not library-as-workers. One of the most resounding messages of COVID-19 is that our field desperately needs to find a way to support one another during times of crisis, including calling out and fighting back against retaliation aimed at workers who are trying to take reasonable measures for their own safety.

VOCATIONAL AWE

The librarian Fobazi Ettarh, in a 2018 article, coined the term *vocational awe*, defining it as the "assumptions librarians have about themselves and the profession that result in beliefs that libraries as institutions are inherently good and sacred, and therefore beyond critique."[11] Many libraries' immediate response to COVID-19 included curbside pickup for patrons who placed holds in advance, which undermined stay-at-home orders and put staff and patrons at undue risk of exposure to the highly contagious coronavirus. It was textbook vocational awe: managers seemed determined to provide this service to uphold reading or demonstrate value to their funders, even at the risk of their communities' safety. The thought of their libraries using up masks, gloves, and cleaning supplies—in the face of a countrywide shortage of personal protective equipment for first responders and in-home health workers—did appear to raise some of these managers' concerns,[12] and criticism of these choices was not taken well.[13]

Other libraries waited to offer curbside pickup until the threat of the virus began to subside and refined their pickup systems to be as contactless as possible. Still, the push to offer regular library services during the height of a deadly pandemic is just the latest example of a long-standing trend of library workers being expected to do more with less (remember the shoestring mentality we told you to abandon?) and to put their needs aside to meet those of others. We need to put a stop to this martyr complex, and that requires unpacking the effects of pressuring our untrained or unprepared colleagues to provide disaster relief. Do we want to keep living in a world where library workers pick up every last task that falls to us through cracks in the social safety net, or do we want to reject it and push our community leaders to build a better future for all?

NOTES

1. David Chanen, "Hennepin County Opens Third Shelter for Homeless in Hotel," *Star Tribune*, April 3, 2020, www.startribune.com/hennepin-county-opens-third-shelter-for-homeless-in-hotel/569362052/.
2. Caitlin Rivers et al., *Public Health Principles for a Phased Reopening during COVID-19: Guidance for Governors* (Baltimore, MD: Johns Hopkins Center for Health Security, April 17, 2020), www.centerforhealthsecurity.org/our-work/publications/public-health-principles-for-a-phased-reopening-during-covid-19-guidance-for-governors.
3. Leah Rosenbaum, "Johns Hopkins Changed Its Guidance on Re-opening the Economy after Pushback from Librarians," *Forbes*, April 23, 2020, www.forbes.com/sites/leahrosenbaum/2020/04/23/johns-hopkins-changed-its-guidance-on-re-opening-the-economy-after-pushback-from-librarians/#249b26c871a2.
4. Antonia Noori Farzan, "A Library Wanted a *New York Times* Subscription: Officials Refused, Citing Trump and 'Fake News,'" *Washington Post*, November 5, 2019, www.washingtonpost.com/nation/2019/11/05/new-york-times-citrus-county-florida-library-subscription-rejected-fake-news/.
5. Lynn Neary, "You May Have to Wait to Borrow a New E-book from the Library," Book News and Features, NPR, November 1, 2019, www.npr.org/2019/11/01/775150979/you-may-have-to-wait-to-borrow-a-new-e-book-from-the-library.
6. American Library Association, "Ensuring #eBooksForAll through America's Libraries" (Policy paper, February 2020), https://ebooksforall.org/wp-content/uploads/2020/02/eBooks_policy_1-pager_02-05-20_WEB.pdf.
7. Carmi Parker, "Editorial: Why We Choose to Boycott Macmillan E-books," *Publisher's Weekly*, November 8, 2019, www.publishersweekly.com/pw/by-topic/industry-news/libraries/article/81688-editorial-why-we-are-boycotting-macmillan-e-books.html.
8. Matt Enis, "Macmillan Ends Library Ebook Embargo," *Library Journal*, March 18, 2020, www.libraryjournal.com/?detailStory=macmillan-ends-library-ebook-embargo.
9. Sean Hollister, "Samsung Quits Making New Blu-ray Players," *The Verge*, February 17, 2019, www.theverge.com/2019/2/17/18228584/samsung-stops-producing-blu-ray-players.
10. Chanen, "Hennepin County Opens Shelter."
11. Fobazi Ettarh, "Vocational Awe and Librarianship: The Lies We Tell Ourselves," *In the Library with the Lead Pipe*, January 10, 2018, www.inthelibrarywiththeleadpipe.org/2018/vocational-awe/.
12. Olivia Solon, "Library Workers Fight for Safer Working Conditions Amid Coronavirus Pandemic," *NBC News*, April 8, 2020, www.nbcnews.com/news/us-news/library-workers-fight-safer-working-conditions-amid-coronavirus-pandemic-n1179346.
13. Zachary Oren Smith, "Coralville Library Board Continues Curbside Book Service, Say They've Changed," *Iowa City Press-Citizen*, April 16, 2020, www.press-citizen.com/story/news/2020/04/16/coralville-library-board-continues-curbside-book-service-say-theyve-changed/5146035002/.

Epilogue

It's Never Perfect and It's Never Done

There are two things we think are most important for librarians to realize about change before they start running out and trying to make it happen. One is that in order to drive change, we need a lot more help from folks underrepresented in our field, in terms of demographics as well as employment backgrounds. By siloing ourselves and leaving our traditions intact, we do our communities a disservice and limit the amount of change we can ever effect. It's well past the time to rethink the requirement of an advanced degree in library and information science for professional librarianship. The soaring costs of education for graduate school, let alone the undergraduate degrees required for admission to it, are an enormous barrier to entry. When the average starting salary for a public librarian can fall below the attendance costs of a master's program,[1] the return on investment is questionable, especially given the number of practicing librarians who will eagerly tell you the number of crucial things they didn't hear a word about in grad school.

The second thing is that our work is never done because change will never stop happening. While researching this book, we skimmed through ALA books published in the past twenty years: *The Accidental Systems Librarian*, *Academic Libraries as High-Tech Gateways*, *The Ultimate Digital Library*, and on and on. These books included fear of and excitement for the world we live in now, and the times we live in are, fittingly enough, scary and exciting. Before COVID-19, we would have told you that the time we've reached in librarianship is an exciting one. Our relevance has stood up to the tests of Amazon and Google, and we continue to redefine our identity, redesign our buildings and services, and demonstrate our value as trusted sources of information—some might say we're entering a renaissance. But as William Gibson has said, "The future is already here. It's just not very evenly distributed." There are libraries in the country that are fighting to stay open, hundred-year-old Carnegie libraries with no HVAC systems, and now unknown numbers of library workers who are filing for unemployment. We have to be scared so we can rally and fight back against these threats. We have to be excited so we can keep our heads in the game and remember the two key things that made many of us choose this work in the first place: helping people and providing equal access to information.

What happens when you perform an image search for *librarian*? At the time of this writing, on both Google and DuckDuckGo you get Carla Hayden and a whole bunch of white people with a few people of color and then a lot more white people. They're all standing in front of books. Some of them are young and sexy, some of them are doing storytimes, some are pushing book trucks, but there's not a single photo without books and bookshelves. We've got nothing against books, but there are so many more kinds of people we need to help shape libraries into the user-centered community hubs we dream about: event planners, marketers, makerspace volunteers, employees from councils on aging and public health, technologists, English language teachers, musicians, and tutors, just to name several. How might we get there? And how might we do a better job of reframing our public image to match all that we know we already do? We hope this book will inspire you to try to answer these questions and come up with questions of your own to ask others, including us.

One of the most difficult stages in a major library construction project happens when the architects and contractors are done, the building is open to the public, and the staff and public have moved into their new home. Everyone expects the multi-million-dollar edifice to be beautiful, efficient, and, well, perfect. It's not. Every building has flaws. Some desired features are eliminated through value engineering (a euphemism for cost cutting), some are overlooked, and some are just plain wrong. Just when everyone has breathed a sigh of relief that the project is complete, this difficult process of discovering these flaws as well as learning the idiosyncrasies of all the new systems and procedures takes at least a year. This is radical change, and it comes on top of years of planning, overwork, and stress. Lauren tries to counsel library directors about the fact that the project isn't done when the doors open, but it's always a shock nonetheless.

The way we learn to live with constant change and our rapidly evolving service role as librarians is by accepting that nothing's ever done, nothing's ever perfect, and, sooner or later, *everything* will change. We have to live with unfinished projects and with a whole lot of uncertainty. It can be enormously challenging, and it's often uncomfortable.

To say we're living in uncertain times is an understatement, but we know that coming to terms with that uncertainty and embracing it are vital right now. In *Emergent Strategy: Shaping Change, Changing Worlds*, adrienne maree brown writes:

> A first question to ask ourselves is, how do we practice increasing our ease with what is? Change happens. Change is definitely going to happen, no matter what we plan or expect or hope for or set in place. We will adapt to that change, or we will become irrelevant.[2]

Adapting to change is like riding the crest of a wave: not tipping over too far into the chaos of future speculation but also not falling back into the backwaters of tradition—a true balancing act. It's exhilarating and overwhelming and scary and fun. It takes passion, patience, and fortitude. And it's where library magic happens.

NOTES

1. Public Libraries, "Average Librarian Salary," January 10, 2012, https://publiclibraries.com/blog/average-librarian-salary/; Best Colleges, "Master's in Library Science Program Guide," www.bestcolleges.com/features/masters-library-science-programs/.
2. brown, adrienne maree, *Emergent Strategy: Shaping Change, Changing Worlds* (Oakland, CA: AK Press, 2017).

Index

CPSIA information can be obtained
at www.ICGtesting.com
Printed in the USA
LVHW042303141121
703275LV00005B/9